POEMS OF GOETHE

POEMS OF
GOETHE

A SELECTION
WITH INTRODUCTION
AND NOTES BY

RONALD GRAY

*Fellow of Emmanuel College and
Lecturer in German in the
University of Cambridge*

CAMBRIDGE
AT THE UNIVERSITY PRESS
1966

CAMBRIDGE UNIVERSITY PRESS
Cambridge, New York, Melbourne, Madrid, Cape Town,
Singapore, São Paulo, Delhi, Mexico City

Cambridge University Press
The Edinburgh Building, Cambridge CB2 8RU, UK

Published in the United States of America by Cambridge University Press, New York

www.cambridge.org
Information on this title: www.cambridge.org/9781107609143

First published 1966
Re-issued 2013

A catalogue record for this publication is available from the British Library

ISBN 978-1-107-60914-3 Paperback

'Bis dann zuletzt des vollen Mondes Helle...'

IN MEMORY OF
HUMPHRY TREVELYAN

CONTENTS

Preface *page* ix

Some views of Goethe's poetry xi

Introduction

 Goethe's life and works xiii

 Goethe's language xviii

THE POEMS

Young Goethe in love 1

Woods and lakes 27

Genius or demi-god 39

Humorous and light verse 73

'Weltanschauungslyrik' 83

Early folk-songs and ballads 97

'Freudvoll und leidvoll' 111

Italian Journey 123

Later narrative poems and ballads 133

Love-poems of his old age 153

Poetry of wisdom 175

Poems of his old age 189

Index of titles and beginnings of poems 197

This selection has been prepared simultaneously with a critical introduction to Goethe's works by the present editor, to be published shortly. The two volumes, though each an entity, are designed to be mutually complementary.

PREFACE

The full editions of Goethe's poems run to a thousand pages
or more, but contain a good deal of occasional verse. The
present volume offers about a hundred poems, mostly grouped
thematically, and suggesting as much as possible of Goethe's
range. (There is none of his 'scientific' poetry, no epic or
dramatic poetry, and only a sample of his verses in classical
metre.) Some very well-known poems are included because
the English-speaking reader should certainly also know them,
although occasionally the esteem in which they are held owes
something to piety. In general, I have chosen what I think the
finest of all Goethe's poems, with an occasional foil of poorer
quality to set them off. The notes are meant to give both help
in understanding the words, and a critical commentary which
I hope will at least stimulate other individual readings. Bio-
graphical notes are as few as possible.

FURTHER READING

The two best annotated editions of Goethe's poems in German
are by Emil Staiger and Erich Trunz. Professor Staiger's, in
three volumes of the 'Manesse Bibliothek' series, follows
almost entirely the ordering of the poems in the 'Ausgabe
letzter Hand', authorized by Goethe himself, but does not
include the *West-östlicher Divan*. Professor Trunz's forms
two volumes in his 'Hamburger Ausgabe' of Goethe's
Works, and arranges the poems more thematically. Of the
two, Professor Staiger writes more for the reader who simply
seeks to enjoy, while Professor Trunz supplies more of the
information needed by the student and scholar. Both kinds of
reader will benefit from the many discussions of poems in
Professor Staiger's three-volume study, *Goethe*, published by
Atlantisverlag, Zürich. For Goethe's own comments on his
poems the 'Conversations with Eckermann' (Everyman's

Library) are useful, or the compendious 'Goethe über seine Dichtungen' by H. G. Gräf. The fullest critical edition is known as the Weimar or the Sophia Edition.

For a general account of Goethe in English there is still nothing better than the *Life*, by G. H. Lewes, reprinted in Everyman's Library. The standard biography in German is that by A. Bielschowsky (revised edition 1928), but the briefer one by Günther Müller is increasing in popularity.

TEXT

The edition by H. G. Gräf in the Inselverlag, 'Goethes Gedichte in zeitlicher Folge', has been taken as a guide, but in a number of cases, especially in the earlier poems, the text of MSS reprinted by Erich Trunz in the 'Hamburger Ausgabe' has been preferred, as being livelier in some cases than the later revisions. In doubtful cases the lists of variant readings in the Weimar Edition have been consulted. I am grateful to Mr Kenneth Rimmer of Haileybury College for help in revising the typescript and advice on the kind of notes which comparative beginners in German would be likely to find most useful.

R. D. G.

Cambridge
July 1965

SOME VIEWS OF GOETHE'S POETRY

In his ballads and lighter lyrics Goethe is most excellent. It is impossible to praise him too highly in this respect. COLERIDGE in *Table Talk* for 1833

Goethe is the greatest poet of modern times, not because he is one of the half-dozen human beings who in the history of our race have shown the most signal gift for poetry, but because, having a very considerable gift for poetry, he was at the same time, in the width, depth, and richness of his criticism of life, by far our greatest modern man. He may be precious and important to us on this account above men of other and more alien times, who as poets rank higher. Nay, his preciousness and importance as a clear and profound modern spirit, as a master-critic of modern life, must communicate a worth of their own to his poetry, and may well make it erroneously seem to have a positive value and perfectness as poetry, more than it has. It is most pardonable for a student of Goethe, and may even for a time be serviceable, to fall into this error. Nevertheless, poetical defects, where they are present, subsist, and are what they are.
MATTHEW ARNOLD in *Mixed Essays*, 1880

Let the candidate fill his mind with the finest cadences he can discover, preferably in a foreign language, so that the meaning of the words may be less likely to divert his attention from the movement; e.g. Saxon charms, Hebridean Folk Songs, the verse of Dante, and the lyrics of Shakespeare—if he can dissociate the language from the cadence. Let him dissect the lyrics of Goethe coldly into their component sound values, syllables long and short, stressed and unstressed, into vowels and consonants. It is not necessary that a poem should rely on its music, but if it does rely on its music that music must be such as will delight the expert.
EZRA POUND in *Pavannes and Divisions*, 1918

We may for instance speak justly enough of the poetry of Goethe as constituting a classic, because of the place which it occupies in its own language and literature. Yet, because of its partiality, of the impermanence of some of its content, and the germanism of its sensibility; because Goethe appears, to a foreign eye, limited by his age, by his language, and by his culture, so that he is unrepresentative of the whole European tradition, and, like our own nineteenth-century authors, a little provincial, we cannot call him a *universal* classic. He is a universal author, in the sense that he is an author with whose works every European ought to be acquainted: but that is a different thing.
T. S. ELIOT in *What is a Classic?*, 1944

As a lyric poet Goethe combines simplicity of utterance with so complete a mastery of verbal music that the most banal ideas become as moving as the faces and objects which form the chosen ambience of our lives. No poet with a less assured technique, and less emotional conviction, could afford to be as obvious as Goethe is, in poem after poem. Verse-making was to him a form of communication almost as effortless as speech....And the result is never facile or vulgar because the idea or emotion is the direct result of an experience, not a conceit chosen as likely to produce an effective poem....It must be admitted that the later proliferations of romantic and symbolist theory have tended to obscure one of the most valuable functions of poetry: the illumination of the usual. It is in this field, above all, that Goethe reigns supreme.

EDWARD SACKVILLE-WEST in *The New Statesman*, 1949

Goethe ist noch immer der am meisten umstrittene Dichter Deutschlands. Daß Kleist oder Hölderlin oder Stifter uns Heutige unmittelbar angehen, scheint allgemein angenommen zu werden. Lessing, Schiller, die meisten Romantiker gelten als Vergangenheit, die man je nachdem museal zu pflegen oder beiseitezuschieben geneigt ist. Nur bei Goethe wird die Frage: Hat er uns heute noch etwas zu sagen? so leidenschaftlich verneint wie bejaht.

EMIL STAIGER in *Goethe*, 1957

INTRODUCTION

Johann Wolfgang Goethe (von Goethe from 1782) was born on 28 August 1749 in Frankfurt am Main, the son of a patrician family, his well-to-do father being a lawyer by education, and his grandfather Chief Magistrate of the city, that is to say, its chief dignitary. He spent the whole of his childhood in Frankfurt and received a private education; he began to write poetry in several languages at a very early age, visited the French theatre often during the occupation of the town by the French in the Seven Years War, and acquired a wide knowledge of classical and modern literature.

In 1765 Goethe matriculated at the University of Leipzig, a city then known as a 'little Paris', where he was taught by, among others, the critic Gottsched and the poet Gellert, both well-known representatives of the rationalistic, Francophile school dominant in Germany at the time, and known as the 'Aufklärung', or 'Enlightenment'. He was known in Leipzig as something of a dandy; his poetry was anacreontic and sometimes erotic; his dramatic writing was strongly influenced by French models, Corneille and Molière. Already, however, he was getting to know the movement towards a more Germanic style in literature: the poet Klopstock, one of its chief exponents, roused his admiration, and he made a first acquaintance with some of the work of Shakespeare, whom Lessing had cited as a better model for German writers than any of the French dramatists. In 1768 he fell ill and had to return home, where he was strongly influenced by a middle-aged woman, Susanna von Klettenberg, a 'Pietist' belonging to a sect akin to the Quakers in some ways. With her he studied alchemy and mysticism, Swedenborg and Paracelsus.

Recovered, Goethe matriculated in 1770 at Strasbourg, to study Law. In the nearby village of Sesenheim he fell in love

with the parson's daughter, Friederike Brion, to whom several of his best-known love-poems, the 'Sesenheimer Lieder', are addressed. In Strasbourg itself, he was influenced by his friend Herder, a leading figure in the anti-rationalistic school later known as 'Sturm und Drang'. Herder taught Goethe to admire Shakespeare, the 'Celtic' poetry of Macpherson, thought at that time to have been written by the primitive bard Ossian, the mystical writings of Hamann ('der Magus im Norden'), Gothic architecture, and folk-poetry, in all of which the most prized quality was the absence of logical orderliness, the untrammelled expression of emotions, the dynamic, apparently chaotic profusion.

In 1771 Goethe returned to Frankfurt as an advocate, with the title of Doctor, abandoning Friederike, a breach of faith for which he felt remorse long afterwards. In the next few months he wrote the essays 'Von deutscher Baukunst', praising the cathedral at Strasbourg for its German qualities, and 'Zum Shakespeare-Tag'; he also wrote, in imitation of Pindar, the rhapsodic poem 'Wanderers Sturmlied'.

During the next few years Goethe swiftly achieved fame. He had spent part of the year 1772 at Wetzlar, where he met Charlotte Buff, who was shortly to marry Johann Kestner. His novel, *Die Leiden des jungen Werther*, published in 1774 and based on this acquaintanceship, was a sensational success throughout Europe. Its themes, those of Werther's hopeless passion for Charlotte and of his spiritual discontent, which together lead him to suicide, caught the mood of young people in unparalleled fashion. Goethe himself, however, was far from being a prisoner of that mood, as is seen from his play *Götz von Berlichingen*, published in 1773. This work, based on the autobiography of a robber-baron of the sixteenth century, and meant as a kind of Shakespearean history, is a plea for heroic self-assertion against pettifogging officialdom, and earned Goethe almost as much fame as *Werther*. *Egmont*, another play begun on Shakespearean lines, was not completed for some years to come. *Faust*, later to be Goethe's best known work, still existed only as an impressive fragment.

At this period Goethe was also moving decisively away from the Christian faith in which he had been brought up. He was much influenced by the philosopher Spinoza, whom he interpreted as a pantheist, studied the Koran and planned a play on Mohammed, and wrote the poem 'Prometheus', expressing defiance of the gods. Despite his opposition to convention, however, love for the society beauty Lili Schönemann, to whom he became engaged in April 1775, almost drew him back into the social world he had come to despise.

A journey of some months to Switzerland, almost immediately after the engagement, was followed by its dissolution. Shortly after, in November 1775, the decisive moment in Goethe's life came when he accepted the invitation of Carl August, Duke of Weimar, to visit him. The visit led to a residence which lasted, with short interruptions, for the whole of the remainder of Goethe's life. He made close friendships with the Duke himself, with the older poet and novelist Wieland, and many others. Above all he came under the calming influence of the wife of Baron von Stein, the Duke's Master of Horse. In Charlotte, Frau von Stein, the 'Lida' of his poetry, Goethe saw an ideal woman, reflected in the central figures of his plays *Iphigenie auf Tauris* and *Torquato Tasso*, begun three or four years after his arrival in Weimar. At her persuasion, he also began to move away from the emotional excesses of 'Sturm und Drang' to a classical simplicity and serenity. For the next ten years, Goethe settled to a quieter and more practical life, accepting office in the government of the Duchy, engaging in a number of serious scientific studies, and writing a good deal for official occasions and entertainments.

Suddenly, on 3 September 1786, while on leave in Karlsbad (in Bohemia), Goethe abandoned all his former society and without informing anyone left for Italy, where he was to stay for almost two years. This was the second decisive turningpoint in his life. All through his adult years he had never given up the admiration he had felt for the ancient world since he first read the encomiums of the art-historian Winckelmann, and encountered Homer. Now he travelled throughout Italy

b

from Venice via Rome to Naples and Sicily (the nearest point to Greece he could then safely reach), taking in the feeling of the Roman and Greek civilizations through his senses, experiencing what he often at the time called a rebirth. He re-wrote or completed *Egmont*, *Iphigenie* and *Tasso*, and added scenes to the still fragmentary *Faust*.

On his return Goethe scandalized Frau von Stein by taking into his household a girl of humble origin and no intellectual gifts, Christiane Vulpius, who lived with him as a wife and bore him many children (all but two of whom died in infancy) before he publicly married her in 1806. It was for Christiane, and mainly about Christiane, that Goethe wrote the poems in imitation of Ovid and others, the *Römische Elegien*, originally entitled *Erotica Romana*. For many years from now onwards, Goethe lived a more domesticated life, and his poetry became more and more an attempt at recreating the poetry of the Greeks, reaching its climax in the Homeric epic on a contemporary theme, *Hermann und Dorothea*.

Meanwhile, Goethe had published in 1790 the greater part of what he had written on the Faust legend, under the title *Faust, ein Fragment*, and the first of his botanical studies, followed by the first of his contributions to optics, in 1791. He remained subject, however, to a certain despondency, caused in part by the horrors of the French Revolution, until the dramatist Schiller, ten years his junior, offered him in 1794 the encouragement of his admiration. The ensuing friendship, lasting until Schiller's death in 1805, resulted first in a revived determination to complete the novel *Wilhelm Meisters Lehrjahre* (begun some fifteen years before, as the *Theatralische Sendung*), which was published in 1795-6 and became the second pillar of Goethe's whole work, alongside *Faust*. There followed a series of ballads in 1797, in a joint venture with Schiller to raise the level of popular taste, and the epigrams known as the *Xenien*, also written with Schiller, and satirizing their common opponents.

Three important works followed after Schiller's death, the First Part of *Faust*, published in 1808, the novel *Die Wahlver-*

wandtschaften (1809), and the *Zur Farbenlehre* (1810), the first full exposition of Goethe's richly symbolical theories on the nature of colour. It was also within this period that Goethe became impressed with the personality of Napoleon, whom he met at Erfurt in 1808.

The next four or five years were a fallow period, during which Goethe, now entering on his sixties, began to compose his autobiographies, the chief of them being *Dichtung und Wahrheit*. However, any notion that his creative life had ended was refuted by the sudden outburst of poetic imagination in 1814 which, increased by his love for the youthful Marianne von Willemer, continued for some five years more and ended as the collection or cycle of poems known as the *West-östlicher Divan*, written for the most part in imitation or emulation of the Persian poet Hafiz. Nor was this the last of Goethe's loves, for there yet remained his passion for the eighteen-year-old Ulrike von Levetzow, for whom he wrote the 'Marienbader Elegie' of 1823.

The final years saw the completion first of the Wilhelm Meister cycle, of which the sequel, known as the *Wanderjahre*, appeared in 1821, to be revised in 1829. Then followed the last assault on the work which had perhaps first occupied Goethe's mind in his youth at Leipzig and at which he had worked intermittently ever since. From 1825 until 1831 (his eighty-first year), Goethe wrote the greater part of the Second Part of *Faust*, holding back its publication until after his death so that it became almost his legacy. He still continued with his scientific works; some of his finest lyrical poetry comes from these late years; he went on as an administrator in the Duchy, and made his home in Weimar a centre of European letters and culture so long as he remained alive. He died, still robust in physique, on 22 March 1832. Legend has it that his dying words were: 'More light!'

The quality of poetry is so constantly present in it, investing every thought with further complexities of sense, that no commentator can hope to do more than give occasional hints or reminders. The commentator is here like a conference interpreter, conveying the speaker's meaning in another language, but losing much of his personality, and above all changing his voice. It is this voice of the poet which we are attempting to hear when we read his poetry, the re-created voice coming out of the printed words he has had set on the page. The poem is like a musical score, and we have not read it properly until we have heard that voice, any more than we have read a score properly until it has sounded, whether in imagination or in reality, in terms of instruments in performance.

The voice of some poets remains the same throughout their lives—there are certain characteristics which mark their work as theirs, regardless of the content. With Goethe this is not so. His range is so wide that it is sometimes scarcely credible that two nevertheless well-authenticated passages could possibly have come from the same hand. In the course of over seventy years as a writer of verses, he changed considerably, and not only from the childlike chanting of this, written at the age of seven:

> Erhabner Groß-Papa! Ein Neues Jahr erscheint,
> Drum muß ich meine Pflicht und Schuldigkeit entrichten...

to this resonant, passionate verse written when he was not far off eighty:

> Sie fehlte ja! mein emsig Tun und Streben,
> Für sie allein ertrug ich's durch die Glut
> Der heißen Stunde; welch erquicktes Leben
> Am kühlen Abend! lohnend war's und gut.

It is true that, in the second passage, something fairly constant in Goethe's mature poetry makes itself felt—the quality of some of the vowels, in their particular contexts, which gives his

statements a good deal of serene power. It is from feeling the force of these in such words as 'lohnend war's und gut', and comparing them with, say, 'des vollen Mondes Helle' and 'Vergönnest mir, in ihre [der Natur] tiefe Brust | Wie in den Busen eines Freunds zu schauen' that one gains some sense of Goethe's open-eyed presence. This is the verbal equivalent of the portrait by Lips in which Goethe appears so broad-faced, so frank and open in his whole expression that one can appreciate the reasons for the goodwill he encountered almost everywhere as a young man, from men and women alike. But while this recurs at most stages of Goethe's life, there is also much in his poetry that changes. He commands ferocity in 'Der Winter und Timur', jaunty insouciance in 'Volk und Knecht…', adoring fervour in 'Ganymed'; he can be intimate and also speak like a prophet, he can be scurrilous and lofty, sentimental and sarcastic, comical and humorous, coarse and melodious, and he writes in most of the metres and verse-forms known in modern Europe.

At the start of his poetic career—that is, when he ceased writing his 'exercise' alexandrines and fashionable anacreontics—Goethe recognized, as Shakespeare had done, the need to write poetry in a language which in some sense could be called colloquial. The theory of the 'Sturm und Drang' might talk of the Genius, and the demi-god poet-creator; what mattered for poetry was the movement's insistence on naturalness, which produced the vividness of some of the dialogue in *Kabale und Liebe* and in Lenz's *Die Soldaten*. The astonishing liberation which Goethe brought to German verse around 1770 was largely due to his ability to let himself go, to use such words as were not considered suitable either for poetry or for literature, and to make them part of his natural rhythms. There was not only what has come to be called 'das grobe Goethe-Wort', or 'das Götz-Wort', there were also dialect words like 'krapelt' and 'spude dich' and 'schlockernd', there were words of his own invention like 'bleit' and 'häkelt' and 'seitblickt', and compounds suggesting extreme carefreeness in their conception: 'Morgenschlossenwolken', and 'Knabenmorgenblütenträume'.

There were rhymes which made no disguise of the fact that Goethe's native speech was that of a citizen of Frankfurt: 'neige' with 'Schmerzensreiche', 'Freuden' with 'beiden', 'ihr' with 'dafür'. All this was an essential breaking-down of inhibitions which had enclosed the German language for decades and had made almost all German poetry in the eighteenth century sound priggish and prim, or at best over-polite. The language of a particular individual, Goethe asserted, was capable of becoming poetry; by implication the language of ordinary people, the colloquial language of his day, was equally suitable.

It was not always a matter of colloquialisms. Sometimes Goethe was more concerned with giving vent to his hot emotion than with the precise observation of other people's speech. Then he would slap down words on the page without thought of syntax: 'Frisch den holpernden | Stock Wurzeln Steine den Trott | Rasch in's Leben hinein', and 'aus dem krampfigen Starren Erdetreibens' and 'Hoch flog | Siegdurchglühter | Jünglinge Peitschenknall, | Und sich Staub walzt', | Wie vom Gebirg herab | Kieselwetter ins Tal...'. If we can take his fragment on the Wandering Jew as containing a confession, he would jump out of bed at midnight 'wie ein Toller' and write with a broomstick if necessary, once the fit was on him: 'Denn es ist Drang, und so ists Pflicht.' To such moods we owe the opening lines of 'An Schwager Kronos', the almost incomprehensible 'Wanderers Sturmlied' and such thick, choked lines as these on the very subject of 'Sprache', as their title indicates:

> Was reich und arm! Was stark und schwach!
> Ist reich vergrabner Urne Bauch?
> Ist stark das Schwert im Arsenal?
> Greif milde drein, und freundlich Glück
> Fließt, Gottheit, von dir aus!...

This was indeed Goethe's view of language in the early 1770's —it was useless, neither rich nor poor, strong nor weak, so long as it stayed buried; only by plunging in ('milde' had the

sense of 'generously' in Goethe's day) could language be made to flow out—and this, moreover, as we guess from 'Kenner und Künstler', in a sense almost sexually metaphorical. With such a view of poetic composition as is implied in that poem, Goethe could sometimes supply an urgent stress, an almost groaning thrust to his words, as he does in the poem written in Autumn 1775:

Fetter grüne, du Laub,
Das Rebengeländer,
Hier mein Fenster herauf,...

or in 'Ganymed':

Ach, an deinem Busen
Lieg' ich, schmachte,
Und deine Blumen, dein Gras
Drängen sich an mein Herz.

or in the lines originally written for Gretchen in the early version of *Faust:*

Mein Schoß, Gott! drängt
Sich nach ihm hin.

The violence with which these monosyllables are wrung from the speaker is something not typical of colloquial speech, and yet close enough to it to reveal one of its potentialities. We know from Luther's verse that German is capable of such a powerful tread, and yet that fact had almost been forgotten by Goethe's day, and it needed his genius to restore the knowledge of it. True, Luther's power came from his belief in Jehovah, while Goethe's came from belief in his own genius and virility. The difference, linguistically speaking, is difficult to detect, although just detectable.

Equally uninhibited was Goethe's way of treating the loftiest concepts as normal parts of daily life, as though they were familiar acquaintances. It takes some time, as a rule, before a reader appreciates that the lines which begin so casually 'Warum gabst du uns die tiefen Blicke' are spoken to Destiny —that this is the 'du' so intimately addressed. Again, in 'An den Mond' the confidential opening 'Füllest wieder Busch und

Tal' is spoken as though to an intimate friend rather than to the moon. Indeed the endearments are so frequent at times—'liebe Nebel', 'liebe Lili' and even 'liebe Liebe'—that in later life Goethe was inclined to substitute some other word when revising for publication.

For some ten years Goethe was able to remain content with this exploratory, liberating use of language. He was doing what needs continually to be done, bringing poetry back from the crystallized forms which it is constantly reassuming, and at the same time revealing qualities of German which we now know to have been there but which could have vanished from hearing. He was also aware, as the final lines of 'Sprache' make plain, that in doing so he was contributing to a national consciousness: 'Faß an zum Siege, Macht, das Schwert, | Und über Nachbarn Ruhm!' Yet his sense of leading Germany into new and better ways of life, heralded in his play *Götz*, inevitably remained dissatisfied by his purely individual self-giving. For a time he could afford to write only in free rhythms and 'Knittelverse' or 'Volkslied' measure, as the mood took him. But just as he found himself needing to accept the restrictions imposed by society, if he was to have any hope of leading it, so he found himself more and more in need of forms, traditional moulds in which to express more complex issues. Certain rhythms begin to establish themselves, evidently unconsciously, in his free verse; he adopts blank verse, and occasionally the discredited alexandrine slips in. Echoes of the Italian stanza begin to appear—they are not quite 'ottave rime' to begin with, but they are hendecasyllabics, and the rhyme-scheme begins to approximate to the Italian form. Before long the hexameter and the pentameter, and later iambic trimeters, 'terza rima' and sonnets emerge. Goethe is attempting to submit his speech to the discipline of the regularly recurring rhyme, with its variety of significant echoes, to the metre which supplies a counterpoint and thereby an implicit comment on his natural rhythms, to make his language ultimately more expressive than it could be while it remained untrammelled.

Yet on the whole these attempts remain less successful than one would have wanted them to be. The alexandrines which come more and more frequently in the course of 'Ilmenau' are not childlike, as are those which begin 'Erhabner Groß-Papa', but they are a reversion to the confined spirit of the earlier eighteenth century, without any new impetus of life. Goethe's hexameters also reflect his difficulties of adaptation. The quantitative measure, whatever modifications were made to suit the accented German language, constantly led him into requiring false emphases, so that the reader is often not so much enjoying the counterpoint of metre and rhythm as scanning a line once again to see where a natural stress must be ignored. Goethe was more successful with 'terza rima', which he used far less often, and which was in any case a matter of rhyme rather than of metre and thus did not present the same difficulties as the hexameter. His sonnets belong to a very short period in his life, and are also not numerous in comparison with the Greek forms which he used over and over again, from shortly before the Italian Journey of 1786 until his death in 1832.

It is open to question whether the move towards formal exactness was made before Goethe's natural inventiveness had had a chance to display itself to the full. It is also a moot point whether his adherence to form in poetry was connected with his adaptation to life at the court of Weimar, so foreign to the kind of life he had seemed to advocate in *Götz*. Certainly, of the two poems most closely concerned with that adaptation, 'Ilmenau' tends increasingly to use the alexandrine, among lines of blank verse, while 'Zueignung' is the first attempt in a long poem to keep within a traditional form of rigid requirements.

Goethe achieves most, even in the period of his classicizing experiments, in the forms which emerge from his creative mind along with mood and meaning. There is more living movement in 'Cupido, loser, eigensinniger Knabe' than there is in the elegiac couplets written at about the same time, and much more in 'Kennst du das Land', where the rhythms are infinitely complex, pausing, pressing down into depths of longing, lilting again before a turn, and changing in pace

xxiii

from vowel to vowel. In 'Zueignung', despite occasional felicities, the movement is already tending towards that steady beat which characterizes even the ballads of around 1797, and which indicates not so much the acceptance of a discipline as the imposition of one. The form of 'Kennst du das Land', on the other hand, is unique among all Goethe's poems: it has, so to speak, created its own form.

The same cannot be said of another outstanding work of the early Weimar years, 'An den Mond', which has, so far as superficialities go, an ordinary rhyme-scheme and simple quatrain structure. Yet here again the movement is so distinctive that its music remains in the mind as something quite different from that of any other poem in the same form. As for 'Über allen Gipfeln', also from the same period when traditional forms were claiming more and more of Goethe's attention, no account will ever do justice to its musicality—and its form is once again unique, belonging solely to the particular mood that was shaping itself into words at that time.

Similarly, of the poetry of Goethe's old age, among the poems which impress most are 'Dämmrung senkte sich von oben', which precisely repeats the form of a poem from Goethe's anacreontic days but has no other echo, 'In tausend Formen', which approximates very distantly to a Persian 'ghasel', and 'Um Mitternacht ging ich', with its striking refrain, rather than those cast in classical or Italianate forms. In all of these Goethe seems to be creating his form as he goes, just as he did in his 'Sturm und Drang' days (a few exceptions will be mentioned below).

What has been gained for poetry by this will be evident from the titles just cited. On the other hand, one may still properly ask what might have come from the adoption of a firmer general purpose. For, as T. S. Eliot says, there are two tasks which a poet may set himself, and on reflection it does seem that Goethe at least had both in mind. He had, in his first ten years, carried out what Eliot has called the movement towards colloquial speech, from artificiality to simplicity, from stiffness to suppleness; could he do what Shakespeare

did in similar circumstances, fulfilling the other possible task of a poet, 'that of experimenting to see how elaborate, how complicated the music could be made without losing touch with colloquial speech altogether'? (*On Poetry and Poets*, p. 36).

One sees some of this strange music, not unreminiscent of *The Winter's Tale* and other works late in the Shakespearean canon, in snatches of Goethe's own later verse, in such mysterious concatenations of sound as those at the beginning of 'Zwiespalt':

> Wenn links an Baches Rand
> Cupido flötet,
> Im Felde rechter Hand
> Mavors drommetet...

The last of these lines is almost as far from normal German as electronic from orchestral music. But it is perhaps more eccentric than impressive, and the poem from which it comes is trivial as a whole. Similarly, the striking phrase describing narcissi in one of the poems imitative of Chinese verse:

> Leuchtet aus dem Mittelherzen
> Rot gesäumt die Glut der Neigung

—which owes some of its effectiveness to the sensual feeling of the words—is ultimately lost as the poem ends in a modest joke, as though Goethe had sought no more than to provide his 'trouvaille' with a background for display. By contrast, in 'Dämmrung senkte sich', another of the 'Chinese' poems, the criss-cross of sounds in 'schwarzvertiefte Finsternisse' and 'schlanker Weiden Haargezweige' is not only ominous but plays a part in the theme of the whole, which is precisely the confrontation and serene containment of such omens. Indeed one can see the enduring, serene Goethe at work within a mere two lines, as the witch-like darkness continues into the next line, there to give place to the long resonances we have already met in 'lohnend war's' and 'schauen':

> Schwarzvertiefte Finsternisse
> Widerspiegelnd ruht der See.

The outcome of the poem in serenity is already forecast by the sounds alone at the end of this first verse: the pace and rhythm of the last three words allow it to be surmised. Goethe explored sounds in this way nowhere so often as in his dramatic fragment *Pandora*, of 1807. It is here that such combinations as this one, describing a musical instrument, are to be found:

Reich uns ein ehern Rohr,
Zierlich zum Mund gespitzt,
Blätterzart angeschlitzt:
Lauter als Menschensang
Schallet es weit.

The sensual excitation of the two words in the central line is not far removed from the effect of Leontes' line in which he curses his unfaithful wife: 'Gone already! | Inch-thick, knee-deep, o'er head and ears a forkt one!'—that is to say, not that the meaning or even the feeling is at all akin, but that one has the sense of words being used with uncanny newness, much as one might be impressed by a boldly successful stroke of the brush in a painting. At other times in *Pandora*, Goethe perhaps strains too much for this newness: there are times when he can sound pseudo-Wagnerian, although the lines following do still avoid the charge of wilful manliness:

Erde, sie steht so fest!
Wie sie sich quälen läßt!
Wie man sie scharrt und plackt!
Wie man sie ritzt und hackt!
Da solls heraus.
Furchen und Riemen ziehn
Ihr auf dem Rücken hin
Knechte mit Schweiß bemühn;
Und wo nicht Blumen blühn,
Schilt man sie aus.

Only a comparison with the Germanicizing verse of Stefan George in the twentieth century could bring out how much less posing there is in Goethe's lines here. Yet there is, conceivably, just a little, though not so much as in the following passage, also from *Pandora*, which is much closer to George:

Als er tot lag,
Jener Hirt, stürzt
Auch mein Glück hin;
Nun die Rach rast,
Zum Verderb strömt
Sein Geschlecht her.
Das Geheg stürzt,
Und ein Wald schlägt
Mächtge Flamm auf.
Durch die Rauchglut
Siedet Balsam
Aus dem Harzbaum.

For all the striking quality of the last three lines, there is here just so much departure from the normalities of German as makes his language pretentious, its German-ness and its masculinity overdone. 'Rach', 'Verderb' and 'Flamm' sound artificial in these contexts just as George occasionally does. Shakespeare can be just as savagely vigorous, as when he lets Timon say 'Destruction fang mankind!' or when Troilus, speaking of Cressida's perfidy, talks of the 'fractions of her faith, orts of her love, | the fragments, scraps, the bits and greasy relics | Of her o'er-eaten faith...' but the words retain their natural shapes, however hideous the sentiments they express, and the whole is still contained within the blank-verse line, giving a unity and even a beauty. Although they writhe or spit they remain human words, and moreover they have a function within the general sense of the play. Goethe's words, in the last passage quoted, just fail to do that. Yet it is passages like this which show how Goethe was continuing to obey his own watchword, 'Greif milde drein'. He was still looking for the pristine words which would make poetry in the teeth of the philistinism of his times, and he could still find them, as isolated nuggets at least, as he had always been able to do since the age of twenty. He was less capable at this point of welding them into whole poems, as he was able to do, to name only one instance, in 'Dämmrung senkte sich'. *Pandora* itself remained a fragment, and what we have of it is hard to comprehend, though occasional verbal flashes show

what might have come. The 'narcissi' poem, like that other late one, 'Das Beet, schon lockert | Sich's in die Höh', contains no more than a well-set gem. Indeed Goethe often had difficulties in making wholes, not only out of his large-scale works but even of quite short poems. His lack of logic (or deliberate rejection of it) and his fascination with paradoxes (which sometimes turn out to be ordinary contradictions) were partly responsible for this. When as many gaps appear between the thought of one verse and that of the next as there are in 'Das Göttliche' and 'Wiederfinden', it is not surprising if poems containing striking rhythms and phrases end by leaving a sense of dissatisfaction. Part of the responsibility must be allotted, however, to the deliberate inconsequentiality of some of Goethe's late work. In one of his many moods, but by no means a rare one, Goethe was very ready to let himself go, not in the sense of his youthful extravagances, but rather in a kind of aged insouciance, an amoral 'going with the tide' in the belief that to do so was to share in the life of the Zeitgeist and thereby almost of the deity. The effect on Goethe's language has been described by Professor Staiger in his lucid account of the *West-östlicher Divan*. Goethe, the critic contends, had by this time (in his sixties) ceased to think of his public and was consequently inclined to be neglectful in a way scarcely believable in one of his talents.

Derselbe Dichter [Professor Staiger writes] der sich neben Schiller der musterhaftesten Diktion befleißigt und in der Epoche der *Pandora* gewaltsam nach neuen Ausdrucksmöglichkeiten gesucht hat, läßt sich nun in einer geradezu verblüffenden Weise gehen. Wortbildungen wie 'entmantelt' oder 'Blumenflors Gelänge', englische Intarsien wie 'Kriegesthunder' und 'bewhelmen' nehmen sich eigenartig aus. Saloppe Verse wie 'du machest mich kaput', 'dem fehlts an dies, dem fehlts an das' sind ein wenig erschreckend. Reime wie 'Koriandern' auf 'Antichambern' kann man nicht einmal mit dem Frankfurter Dialekt entschuldigen. Und mit Stellen wie 'außer diesen Zelten' (für 'außerhalb dieser Zelte') oder 'mit diesem Lied und Wendung' befreunden sich ernste Grammatiker kaum.

It is generous of Professor Staiger to speak of these as 'behagliche Lizenzen' which lend 'einen verwirrenden Reiz'; less

comprehensible when he adds that they are responsible for producing the sense of entering into 'das köstlichste Eigentum hoch humanistischer Geister deutscher Sprache'. They might be more readily excused because of the quality of other Goethean verse, but to present these very defects as the mark of high quality is contrary to good sense. One is, rather, inclined to regret such elements, not merely because they are what they are, but because they suggest a hamstringing of Goethe's poetic endeavours. In his easeful play Goethe was occasionally too easily persuaded that the phrases which came to him with such astonishing power were sufficient in themselves, or perhaps it would be true to say that he was endowed with such facility that he could afford to use up ideas which a lesser man would have saved up for a special occasion. The *Divan* does contain a score of very remarkable poems including 'Selige Sehnsucht', 'Vollmondnacht', 'Dir mit Wohlgeruch zu kosen' and others already mentioned. Yet too often Goethe would allow a poem to tail off into triviality, or into a kind of shorthand statement of beliefs and attitudes which may well have appeared coherent to him, but whose connection one with another is not made clear to the reader. ('Vermächtnis' is a case in point.)

Some of Goethe's work thus has the fault of its virtue. It was by letting himself go that he found it possible to write with the vitality and originality he displayed throughout a very long life, but it was by letting himself go that he also became neglectful, careless rather than carefree. Compared with the greatest of poets, he did not accomplish the double task of both liberating language and taking it, within disciplined limits, to the farthest verges of the speech known to his contemporaries: he did not as a rule create wholes. In most of his *formal* experiments he moved further and further from the speech of his time, doing violence to it rather than transcending it. All the same, in those moments when his grasping at the source of his being 'came off', his living voice still communicates itself. He could return even to a formal mode of expression successfully if the spirit moved him, as it still did in the

'terza rima' of one of his last and best poems, 'Schillers Reliquien'; or he could himself create the form that conveyed his meaning, as in 'Um Mitternacht'. He is like the sower in the parable: some of his ideas fall on stony ground, but some flourish abundantly, and some do so even when they are not sown broadcast but trained under rigid conditions.

Goethe's verse, then, is a cornucopia, and occasionally something of a lucky dip. It springs from his continual self-renewal, which in turn springs, indeed floods out, from his continual renewal of gratitude for all existence. No one can complain if amid all this profusion, itself only a comparatively small part of the whole of Goethe's works, there are disappointments or even an occasional disaster. Yet while it was the condition of Goethe's greatness that he should pour out the abundance he had in him, we who are his readers and not the livers of his particular life should not neglect to distinguish his highest achievements from the rest. This is, after all, what criticism is about—not a carping refusal to admit great qualities, as it is much too often represented as being, but a vigilant readiness to sort out the diamonds not only from the pebbles but from the paste as well. The commentaries which follow are meant to supply a coherent picture of Goethe's verse with which the reader may or may not find himself agreeing—it would be a dull work if he found himself agreeing all the time. Even within so short a compass it includes poems which are not of the best, in the belief that the most useful introduction to Goethe is not one which creates an impression that he could never go wrong, but one which helps to make clear how well he could succeed, being the kind of man he was. There are two phrases of Goethe's which can justify such an undertaking. The one, spoken by Alphons in *Torquato Tasso*, asserts, 'Es will der Feind, es darf der Freund | Nicht schonen.' The other is a saying of Goethe himself: 'Nur wer mich liebt darf mich tadeln.' With such precepts in mind a reader is unlikely to go wrong.

YOUNG GOETHE
IN LOVE

.

YOUNG GOETHE IN LOVE

Goethe's youthful love-poems are not simply the ones he wrote to girls and women; he is in love in just the same way with the earth, the grass pricking through his shirt and the water rippling over him. Several poems in this anthology which have found their way into other sections might, then, equally well have been put here. They are all part of the delighted high spirits with which Goethe discovers himself to be alive and actually enjoying it. There is often a note of humour about them, as though it were all almost too good to be true, a note which sometimes disappears in the later revisions. There is scarcely anywhere, in the poetry of these early days, any note of longing or disappointment, yearning or unrequited love; there was, of course, in *Werther*. Rather, Goethe seems whole-heartedly glad of the love of one girl after another, yet at the same time glad to retain a part of himself quite independent. In his student days at Leipzig he had already noted the strange fact that he could be happier away from his mistress than with her (see 'Glück der Entfernung', not included here), and this lack of any need for reciprocity, which he felt at times, was to find a parallel expression in the words he gave to the courtesan Philine in *Wilhelm Meister:* 'Wenn ich dich liebe, was geht's dich an?' (Again in *Wilhelm Meister*, Natalie replies to the question whether she has ever loved with the words 'Never, or always'.) There was a detached centre to his being, 'frei von Furcht, zu groß zum Neide', which did not expect requital, and did not always give it. But there was also a generous appreciativeness in him, not only for the simple parson's daughter Friederike Brion at Sesenheim, near Strasbourg, but also for the buxom, hearty girl now known only from the poem entitled 'Auf Christianen R.', the society beauty Lili Schönemann, and later the noble-minded Frau Charlotte von Stein. Goethe had something of the chamaeleon about him,

3 1-2

as he himself observed; perhaps because of his inner detach-
ment he could the more easily adapt himself to the image
formed of him by each new lover. And no doubt his own
sometimes fervent, sometimes amused delight, the warmth
of his acceptance and his appreciation helped to make that
image whatever it happened to be. His enthusiasm almost
created a world in which he could be loved.

* * *

MIT EINEM GEMALTEN BAND

Kleine Blumen, kleine Blätter
Streuen mir mit leichter Hand
Gute junge Frühlings-Götter
Tändelnd auf ein luftig Band.

Zephir, nimms auf deine Flügel,
Schlings um meiner Liebsten Kleid;
Und so tritt sie vor den Spiegel
All in ihrer Munterkeit.

Sieht mit Rosen sich umgeben,
Selbst wie eine Rose jung.
Einen Blick, geliebtes Leben!
Und ich bin belohnt genung.

Fühle, was dies Herz empfindet,
Reiche frei mir deine Hand,
Und das Band, das uns verbindet,
Sei kein schwaches Rosenband!

The fashionable world of Leipzig, the 'klein Paris' which Goethe
encountered at the age of eighteen, thought of love as a teasing sport
between shepherds and shepherdesses in which the 'heiße Triebe' of the
one pleaded for the 'himmlische Vergnügen' at long last blushingly pro-
vided by the other. 'Zärtlichkeit', 'Wollust', 'Entzücken' are the themes
of this pretty, Rococo world, as they are of most of Goethe's poems before
1770.
These verses, written in 1771 at Strasbourg, were sent by Goethe to

Friederike Brion together with, as was the custom, a ribbon on which he had himself painted amoretti scattering roses. Nothing could have been more fashionable. However, despite roses and cupids there is a note which Erich Trunz describes as 'nicht Galanterie sondern Herzlichkeit, schlicht, volksmäßig'. This may be seen from the differences between the version here printed (that of 1789) and the original version, all tending to give increased warmth and intensity. In line 8 Goethe originally had the much less excited 'mit zufriedener Munterkeit'; in line 10 he had 'Sie wie eine Rose jung', and in line 14, 'Reich mir deine liebe Hand', which has nothing like the flourish of geniality the present version has.

Beethoven's setting makes these verses unforgettable.

WILLKOMMEN UND ABSCHIED

Es schlug mein Herz, geschwind zu Pferde!
Es war getan fast eh gedacht.
Der Abend wiegte schon die Erde,
Und an den Bergen hing die Nacht;
Schon stand im Nebelkleid die Eiche,
Ein aufgetürmter Riese, da,
Wo Finsternis aus dem Gesträuche
Mit hundert schwarzen Augen sah.

Der Mond von einem Wolkenhügel
Sah kläglich aus dem Duft hervor,
Die Winde schwangen leise Flügel,
Umsausten schauerlich mein Ohr;
Die Nacht schuf tausend Ungeheuer,
Doch frisch und fröhlich war mein Mut:
In meinen Adern welches Feuer!
In meinem Herzen welche Glut!

Dich sah ich, und die milde* Freude
Floß von dem süßen Blick auf mich;
Ganz war mein Herz an deiner Seite
Und jeder Atemzug für dich.
Ein rosenfarbnes Frühlingswetter
Umgab das liebliche Gesicht,

Und Zärtlichkeit für mich — ihr Götter!
Ich hofft es, ich verdient es nicht!

Doch ach, schon mit der Morgensonne
Verengt der Abschied mir das Herz:
In deinen Küssen welche Wonne!
In deinem Auge welcher Schmerz!
Ich ging, du standst und sahst zur Erden,
Und sahst mir nach mit nassem Blick:
Und doch, welch Glück, geliebt zu werden!
Und lieben, Götter, welch ein Glück!

mild: here in the medieval sense, still current in Goethe's day, of 'generous, lavish'.

Written in 1770 or 1771 and meant for Friederike, this vigorous piece is one of Goethe's most obviously 'Sturm und Drang' poems, and yet not wholly in the mood of that hot-headed literary movement of his youth. The version kept by Friederike (printed in Trunz's edition) shows how humorously Goethe had regarded his passionate outburst. The second line, it appears, originally ran 'Und fort, wild wie ein Held zur Schlacht', which is amusing both in its abruptness and in its incongruous simile. In the second line of verse 2 the moon 'sah *schläfrig* aus dem Duft hervor', an unromantic thing to do, and four lines later Goethe had had a retort to the thousand monsters of the night in the words 'Doch tausendfacher war mein Mut', with their 'burschikos' effect. ('Tausend' can have ludicrous associations as in 'ein Tausendsasa'—a 'hell of a guy'—and 'Potztausend!' —'blimey!')

The version printed here, the commonly known one, while retaining something of the original mood, at least in its rhythm, also makes some improvements. The last lines of verse 2 were really 'Sturm und Drang' in their conventional exaggeration when they read 'Mein Geist war ein verzehrend Feuer | Mein ganzes Herz zerfloß in Glut'. The words 'ein aufgetürmter Riese' give more physical impression of height than did the original 'wie ein getürmter Riese'. In verse 3 'umgab' is better than the earlier '*lag auf dem* lieblichen Gesicht', which is inappropriately heavy.

In each version, the feeling is above all of impetuosity, sometimes humorously regarded. The rider is exultant in his power to overcome the night-time terrors, no less exultant at seeing his sweetheart, and scarcely touched at their enforced leave-taking, which he thrusts aside with 'Und doch...'. The last lines were more acceptable, emotionally, when, as in the earlier version, it was the *rider* who stayed behind 'und sah *dir* nach mit

6

nassem Blick'—he might more appropriately say that love was happiness all the same. The revised version, making *him* leave as of course he must have done, also makes him brush aside the girl's tears rather sweepingly. The ecstatic affirmation of the last two lines, still linked by rhyme with the slower lines of the departure, comes too suddenly to be quite convincing.

UNBESTÄNDIGKEIT

Auf Kieseln im Bache, da lieg' ich, wie helle,
Verbreite* die Arme der kommenden Welle,
Und buhlerisch drückt sie die sehnende Brust.
Dann trägt sie ihr Leichtsinn im Strome darnieder,
Schon naht sich die zweite und streichelt mich wieder,
Da fühl' ich die Freuden der wechselnden Lust.

O Jüngling, sei weise, verwein' nicht vergebens
Die fröhlichsten Stunden des traurigen Lebens,
Wenn flatterhaft dich ja ein Mädchen vergißt.
Geh, ruf sie zurücke, die vorigen Zeiten,
Es küßt sich so süße der Busen der zweiten
Als kaum* sich der Busen der ersten geküßt.

Verbreite: 'breite aus'; (the modern sense of 'verbreite' is 'widen'). *Als kaum*: the sense is that the first can scarcely compete with the second.

Written at Leipzig (1768–9). This is the version printed in 1770. That of 1789 was entitled 'Wechsel', and substituted 'eilenden' for the possibly incongruous 'traurigen' in line 8, as well as 'Lippe' for 'Busen' in the last lines. The title seems to be a deliberate flouting of that 'Beständigkeit' which seventeenth-century poets were unanimous in praising.

Erwache, Friederike,
Vertreib die Nacht,
Die einer deiner Blicke
Zum Tage macht.
Der Vögel sanft Geflüster
Ruft liebevoll,
Daß mein geliebt Geschwister*
Erwachen soll.

7

Ist dir dein Wort nicht heilig
Und meine Ruh'?
Erwache! Unverzeihlich —
Noch schlummerst du!
Horch, Philomelens* Kummer
Schweigt heute still,
Weil dich der böse Schlummer
Nicht meiden will.

Es zittert Morgenschimmer
Mit blödem* Licht
Errötend durch dein Zimmer
Und weckt dich nicht.
Am Busen deiner Schwester,
Der für dich schlagt*,
Entschläfst du immer fester,
Je mehr es tagt.

Ich seh' dich schlummern, Schöne!
Vom Auge rinnt
Mir eine süße Träne
Und macht mich blind.
Wer kann es fühllos sehen,
Wer wird nicht heiß,
Und wär' er von den Zehen
Zum Kopf von Eis!

Vielleicht erscheint dir träumend
— O Glück! — mein Bild,
Das halb voll Schlaf und reimend
Die Musen schilt.
Erröten und erblassen
Sieh sein Gesicht:
Der Schlaf hat ihn verlassen,
Doch wacht er nicht.

Die Nachtigall im Schlafe
Hast du versäumt,
So höre nun zur Strafe,
Was ich gereimt.
Schwer lag auf meinem Busen
Des Reimes Joch:
Die schönste meiner Musen,
Du, schliefst ja noch.

mein geliebt Geschwister: 'my beloved sisters', that is, Friederike and *her* sister. *Philomele*: 'the nightingale'. *blöd*: 'pale' (the meaning today is 'stupid'). *schlagt*: 'schlägt'.

From papers given by Friederike's sister to a visitor at Sesenheim three years after Goethe's death. Never published by Goethe, whose authorship has been disputed, this is evidently an impromptu piece. The humour of the ideas and of the rhyme 'heilig/unverzeihlich' (which presupposes a soft 'g' typical of Goethe's native Frankfurt speech) suggests that Goethe may have been the author, perhaps at a moment when his feeling for Friederike was one of amused affection. The verses are put together in a carefree way, it is true, but the poet tells us the reason for this himself.

Balde seh ich Rickchen wieder,
Balde bald umarm ich sie,
Munter tanzen meine Lieder
Nach der süßten Melodie.

Ach, wie schön hats mir geklungen,
Wenn sie meine Lieder sang!
Lange hab ich nicht gesungen,
Lange, liebe Liebe, lang.

Denn mich ängsten tiefe Schmerzen,
Wenn mein Mädchen mir entflieht,
Und der wahre Gram im Herzen
Geht nicht über in ein Lied.

Doch jetzt sing ich, und ich habe
Volle Freude süß und rein.
Ja, ich gäbe diese Gabe
Nicht für aller Klöster Wein.

Also given to a visitor in 1835. The lively beginning and the endearment (Rickchen for Friederikchen), together with the charming emphasis of 'balde bald', speak for Goethe's authorship. So does the suddenly serious note at 'Lange, liebe Liebe, lang'—that is surely Goethe's voice—and the even more serious mention of 'der wahre Gram im Herzen', where the future Werther seems to be speaking. The poem remains a delightful trifle, altogether more amused than deeply concerned with 'Gram', as the reference to cloisters in the last line shows. (Monasteries in Germany do produce wine; Goethe seems, however, to be contrasting the monastic state with his own as a lover.) The full force of his passion for Friederike, caught up in all the splendour of Nature, is to be felt in 'Mailied' (p. 30).

AUF CHRISTIANEN R.

Hab oft einen dummen düstern Sinn,
Ein gar so schweres Blut;
Wenn ich bei meiner Christel bin,
Ist alles wieder gut.
Ich seh sie dort, ich seh sie hier
Und weiß nicht auf der Welt,
Und wie und wo und wann sie mir,
Warum sie mir gefällt.

Das schwarze Schelmenaug' dadrein,
Die schwarzen Brauen* drauf,
Seh ich ein einzigmal hinein,
Die Seele geht mir auf.
Was sie so gar einen süßen Mund,
Liebrunde Wänglein hat!
Ach, und es ist noch etwas rund,
Da sieht kein Aug' sich satt.

Und wenn ich sie dann fassen darf
Im lüft'gen deutschen Tanz,
Da geht's herum, da geht's so scharf,
Da fühl' ich mich so ganz.

Und wenn's ihr tummlig* wird und warm,
Da wieg' ich sie sogleich
An meiner Brust, in meinem Arm —
Ist mir ein Königreich!

Und wenn sie liebend nach mir blickt
Und alles rings vergißt,
Und dann an meine Brust gedrückt
Und weidlich eins geküßt,*
Das läuft mir durch das Rückenmark
Bis in die große Zeh',
Ich bin so schwach, ich bin so stark,
Mir ist so wohl, so weh.

Da möcht' ich mehr und immer mehr,
Der Tag wird mir nicht lang.
Wenn ich die Nacht auch bei ihr wär',
Davor wär' mir nicht bang.
Ich denk', ich fasse sie einmal
Und büße meine Lust;
Und endigt sich nicht meine Qual,
Sterb' ich an ihrer Brust.

Braunen: 'Brauen', 'brows'. *tummlig*: 'taumelig', 'swooning'. *weidlich eins geküßt*:
'weidlich' means 'good and strong'. The absolute past participle lends vividness.

Written not later than 1774. It is not known to whom the lines refer. In
a later version, entitled 'Christel', some of the jollity disappears: line 13
becomes 'Ist eine, die so lieben Mund', losing the relish of the present
irregular metre. The self-depreciating 'dummen' in the first line is changed
to the pleonastic 'dumpfen'.

The jolliness of the poem is in surprising contrast both to the poems
addressed to Lili Schönemann and those to Charlotte von Stein. 'Und
weidlich eins geküßt'—it was a real smacker, by the sound of it. Similarly,
the ecstatic repetitions of the first verse give a rollicking feeling so
unlike the picture one has of Goethe in love at other times that one
wonders whether the poem was dramatic or fictional, although it was
probably not.

NEUE LIEBE, NEUES LEBEN

Herz, mein Herz, was soll das geben,
Was bedränget dich so sehr?
Welch ein fremdes neues Leben —
Ich erkenne dich nicht mehr.
Weg ist alles, was du liebtest,
Weg, worum du dich betrübtest,
Weg dein Fleiß und deine Ruh —
Ach, wie kamst du nur dazu?

Fesselt dich die Jugendblüte,
Diese liebliche Gestalt,
Dieser Blick voll Treu und Güte
Mit unendlicher Gewalt?
Will ich rasch mich ihr entziehen,
Mich ermannen, ihr entfliehen,
Führet mich im Augenblick
— Ach — mein Weg zu ihr zurück.

Und an diesem Zauberfädchen,
Das sich nicht zerreißen läßt,
Hält das liebe lose* Mädchen
Mich so wider Willen fest.
Muß in ihrem Zauberkreise
Leben nun auf ihre Weise;
Die Verändrung, ach, wie groß!
Liebe, Liebe, laß mich los!

lose: 'roguish', 'teasing'.

AN BELINDEN*

Warum ziehst du mich unwiderstehlich,
Ach, in jene Pracht?
War ich guter Junge nicht so selig
In der öden Nacht?

Heimlich in mein Zimmerchen verschlossen
Lag im Mondenschein,
Ganz von seinem Schauerlicht umflossen,
Und ich dämmert' ein.

Träumte da von vollen goldnen Stunden
Ungemischter Lust;
Ahndungsvoll* hatt' ich dein Bild empfunden
Tief in meiner Brust.

Bin ich's noch, den du bei so viel Lichtern
An dem Spieltisch hältst?
Oft so unerträglichen Gesichtern
Gegenüberstellst?

Reizender ist mir des Frühlings Blüte
Nun nicht auf der Flur,
Wo du Engel bist, ist Lieb' und Güte,
Wo du bist, Natur.

Belinden: see commentary below. *Ahndungsvoll*: 'ahnungsvoll', 'with intuitive foreknowledge'.

VOM BERGE

Wenn ich, liebe Lili, dich nicht liebte,
Welche Wonne gäb' mir dieser Blick!
Und doch, wenn ich, Lili, dich nicht liebte,
Fänd' ich hier und fänd' ich dort mein Glück?

All three of these poems were written in 1775, about Lili Schönemann, as was the one following. They all concerned with Goethe's reluctant avowal that he, the author of *Götz von Berlichingen* and apostle of natural freedom, is in love with a society beauty, enslaved to her as much as any townee. 'Neue Liebe, neues Leben' indeed—not simply in the sense that love restores him to life anew but that it restores him to a life he had thought to spurn, the life of salons and card-tables, gossip and foppery. While the rhythm of the first poem begins with almost a groan, there is a humorous desperation in the outcry of the last line.

'An Belinden' takes as its title the name of the heroine of Pope's *Rape of the Lock*, though once again it is Lili that Goethe means. He thinks of the time

when, like Faust, he shut himself up in his room in a romantic moonlight, and dreamt of enjoying beauty unsurpassed. But the Helen he now meets, somewhat to his astonishment, is Lili, and the paradise she offers him is the gaming-room with its candelabras. Fantastically, as he now feels, not even the Spring in the countryside has more attraction for him than Lili has; Nature is Lili, not the fields outside.

Away from Lili's companionship, in 'Vom Berge' which he wrote by Lake Zürich (see the poem on p. 32 below), Goethe muses on his sacrifice. If he had not come to see Nature in Lili, what delight he would have from this hillside view (which probably included a range of the Alps)! But if he did not love Lili, what delight could he possibly have in anything at all? Whereas Nature had enhanced his love of Friederike, his love of Lili now requires him to abandon Nature for her, or to persuade himself that the two are identical. But he is not really committed: there is a humorous note running through all the Lili poems, and from some inward and detached centre he watches his infatuation with a quizzical smile. See Goethe's account near the beginning of Dichtung und Wahrheit, book 17.

LILIS PARK

Ist doch keine Menagerie
So bunt als meiner Lili ihre!
Sie hat darin die wunderbarsten Tiere
Und kriegt sie 'rein, weiß selbst nicht wie.
O wie sie hüpfen, laufen, trappeln,
Mit abgestumpften Flügeln zappeln,
Die armen Prinzen* allzumal,
In nie gelöschter Liebesqual!

'Wie hieß die Fee? Lili?' — Fragt nicht nach ihr!
Kennt ihr sie nicht, so danket Gott dafür.

Welch ein Geräusch, welch ein Gegacker,
Wenn sie sich in die Türe stellt
Und in der Hand das Futterkörbchen hält!
Welch ein Gequiek, welch ein Gequacker!
Alle Bäume, alle Büsche
Scheinen lebendig zu werden:
So stürzen sich ganze Herden

14

Zu ihren Füßen; sogar im Bassin die Fische
Patschen ungeduldig mit den Köpfen heraus.
Und sie streut dann das Futter aus
Mit einem Blick — Götter zu entzücken,
Geschweige die Bestien. Da geht's an ein Picken,
An ein Schlürfen, an ein Hacken;
Sie stürzen einander über die Nacken,
Schieben sich, drängen sich, reißen sich,
Jagen sich, ängsten sich, beißen sich,
Und das all um ein Stückchen Brot,
Das, trocken, aus den schönen Händen schmeckt,
Als hätt es in Ambrosia gesteckt.

Aber der Blick auch! der Ton,
Wenn sie ruft: Pipi! Pipi!
Zöge den Adler Jupiters vom Thron;
Der Venus Taubenpaar,
Ja der eitle Pfau* sogar,
Ich schwöre, sie kämen,
Wenn sie den Ton von weitem nur vernähmen.

Denn so hat sie aus des Waldes Nacht
Einen Bären, ungeleckt und ungezogen,
Unter ihren Beschluß* hereinbetrogen,
Unter die zahme Kompanie gebracht,
Und mit den andern zahm gemacht —
Bis auf einen gewissen Punkt, versteht sich!
Wie schön und ach! wie gut
Schien sie zu sein! Ich hätte mein Blut
Gegeben, um ihre Blumen zu begießen.

'Ihr sagtet: *ich!* Wie? Wer?'
Gut denn, ihr Herrn, grad aus: *Ich* bin der Bär;
In einem Filetschurz* gefangen,
An einem Seidenfaden ihr zu Füßen.
Doch wie das alles zugegangen,
Erzähl' ich euch zur andern Zeit;
Dazu bin ich zu wütig heut'.

Denn ha! steh' ich so an der Ecke
Und hör' von weitem das Geschnatter,
Seh' das Geflitter, das Geflatter,
Kehr' ich mich um
Und brumm',
Und renne rückwärts eine Strecke
Und seh' mich um
Und brumm',
Und laufe wieder eine Strecke,
Und kehr' doch endlich wieder um.

Dann fängt's auf einmal an, zu rasen,
Ein mächt'ger Geist schnaubt aus der Nasen,
Es wildzt* die innere Natur.
Was, du ein Tor, ein Häschen nur!
So ein Pipi!* Eichhörnchen, Nuß zu knacken!
Ich sträube meinen borstgen Nacken,
Zu dienen ungewöhnt.
Ein jedes aufgestutzte Bäumchen höhnt
Mich an! ich flieh' vom Boulingreen,*
Vom niedlich glatt gemähten Grase;
Der Buchsbaum zieht mir eine Nase,
Ich flieh ins dunkelste Gebüsche hin,
Durchs Gehäge zu dringen,
Über die Planken zu springen!
Mir versagt Klettern und Sprung,
Ein Zauber bleit* mich nieder,
Ein Zauber häkelt* mich wider.
Ich arbeite mich ab, und bin ich matt genung,
Dann lieg' ich an gekünstelten Kaskaden
Und kau' und wein' und wälze halb mich tot,
Und ach! es hören meine Not
Nur porzellanene Oreaden.*

Auf einmal! ach, es dringt
Ein seliges Gefühl durch alle meine Glieder!
Sie ists, die dort in ihrer Laube singt!
Ich höre die liebe, liebe Stimme wieder,

Die ganze Luft ist warm, ist blütevoll.
Ach, singt sie wohl, daß ich sie hören soll?
Ich dringe zu, tret' alle Sträuche nieder,
Die Büsche fliehn, die Bäume weichen mir,
Und so — zu ihren Füßen liegt das Tier.
Sie sieht es an: 'Ein Ungeheur! doch drollig!
Für einen Bären zu mild,
Für einen Pudel zu wild;
So zottig, täpsig,* knollig!'*
Sie streicht ihm mit dem Füßchen übern Rücken;
Er denkt im Paradiese zu sein.
Wie ihn alle sieben Sinne* jücken!
Und sie — sieht ganz gelassen drein.
Ich küss' ihre Schuhe, kau' an den Sohlen,
So sittig, als ein Bär nur mag;
Ganz sachte heb' ich mich und schwinge mich verstohlen
Leis an ihr Knie — am günst'gen Tag
Läßt sie's geschehn und kraut mir um die Ohren
Und patscht mich mit mutwillig derbem Schlag;
Ich knurr', in Wonne neu geboren.
Dann fordert sie mit süßem, eitlem Spotte:
'Allons tout doux!* eh la menotte!
Et faites Serviteur,
Comme un joli Seigneur.'
So treibt sie's fort mit Spiel und Lachen!
Es hofft der oft betrogne Tor;
Doch will er sich ein bißchen unnütz machen,*
Hält sie ihn kurz als wie zuvor.

Doch hat sie auch ein Fläschchen Balsam-Feuers,
Dem keiner Erde Honig gleicht,
Wovon sie wohl einmal, von Lieb und Treu erweicht,
Um die verlechzten Lippen ihres Ungeheuers
Ein Tröpfchen mit der Fingerspitze streicht
Und wieder flieht und mich mir überläßt,
Und ich dann, losgebunden, fest
Gebannt bin, immer nach ihr ziehe,

Sie suche, schaudre, wieder fliehe —
So läßt sie den zerstörten Armen gehn,
Ist seiner Lust, ist seinen Schmerzen still;
Ha! manchmal läßt sie mir die Tür halb offen stehn,
Seitblickt* mich spottend an, ob ich nicht fliehen will.

Und ich! — Götter, ists in euren Händen,
Dieses dumpfe Zauberwerk zu enden:
Wie dank' ich, wenn ihr mir die Freiheit schafft!
Doch sendet ihr mir keine Hilfe nieder —
Nicht ganz umsonst reck' ich so meine Glieder:
Ich fühl's! ich schwör's! Noch hab' ich Kraft.

die armen Prinzen: alludes to the companions of Ulysses, whom Circe transformed into
beasts. der eitle Pfau: the peacock was Juno's bird. Beschluß: 'custody' (not 'decision',
the usual sense). Filetschurz: 'Filet' means a kind of crotchet-work; 'Schurz'=
'Schürze', a 'skirt', but here probably a shawl is meant. wildzt: 'goes wild' (word
coined by Goethe). Pipi: a word used for calling to birds; here also used as a noun.
Boulingreen: a French form of the English 'bowling-green'. bleit: 'drags like lead'
or 'hits like a lead bullet' (word coined by Goethe). häkelt: 'holds with a hook'
(word coined by Goethe). Oreaden: in Greek mythology, nymphs of the mountains.
täpsig: 'awkward, clumsy' (more often 'täppisch' or 'tapsig'). knollig: 'boorish, like
a yokel'. alle sieben Sinne: Goethe says seven senses, not five, perhaps for the fun of
alliteration, perhaps by association with 'die sieben Sünden'. Allons tout doux, etc.:
'There's a pretty boy! Giveums ickle paw and bowums head like a nice gentleman.'
sich...unnütz machen: 'get up to his (naughty) tricks'. Seitblickt: 'looks sideways'
(word coined by Goethe).

Written in 1775 about Lili Schönemann, this is one of Goethe's most
zestful and humorous works. There are no variant readings of any con-
sequence; the version here is the earlier one. A passage in *Dichtung und
Wahrheit*, book 19, is relevant.

The whole Rococo world which Goethe had thought to leave behind
him in Leipzig is brought to mind in this poem: the porcelain nymphs of
'Dresden china', the avenues of heavily pruned trees and box-hedges, the
artificial cascades and pools of golden carp, the close-cropped lawns. It is
essentially a cosmopolitan world, as the admixture of foreign words shows:
Bassin, Kompanie, Filetschurz, Boulingreen, Kaskaden, porzellanen—the
world of Versailles which German princes had long been copying, and
which the new generation was violently rejecting. The classical setting in
which Lili appears as the sorceress Circe, and Goethe as one of the suitors
she has transformed into animals, is in keeping with all this.

Goethe is not simply fooling: he feels tenderly at the line 'Ich höre die
liebe, liebe Stimme wieder', and when he adds 'Die ganze Luft ist warm, ist
blütevoll' we may think of his words in another 'Lili' poem: 'Wo du bist,

Natur'. Nowhere in the poem is there any reason to think of Goethe as just one more dandified suitor. Rather, he is genuinely astonished (and amused) at the preposterous situation in which he finds himself. That the situation ever came about is due to Goethe's extraordinary frankness and openness to experience, as much as to anything else. He did not cast himself in the role of a 'Stürmer und Dränger' and stick to that, but was prepared, even within a few years, to return to classicism if need arose, and his devotion to Lili was already the beginning of a return to the world where classicism was the accepted thing. At the same time, his language in this poem is so cheerfully full of colloquialisms, neologisms, and amusing rhythmical devices (especially the vivid 'Kehr' ich mich um | und brumm'...') that the classical references appear only with due disrespect.

RASTLOSE LIEBE

Dem Schnee, dem Regen,
Dem Wind entgegen,
Im Dampf der Klüfte,
Durch Nebeldüfte,
Immer zu! Immer zu!
Ohne Rast und Ruh!

Lieber durch Leiden
Möcht ich mich schlagen,
Als so viel Freuden
Des Lebens ertragen.
Alle das Neigen
Von Herzen zu Herzen,*
Ach, wie so eigen
Schaffet das Schmerzen!

Wie — soll ich fliehen?*
Wälderwärts ziehen?
Alles vergebens!
Krone des Lebens,
Glück ohne Ruh,
Liebe, bist du!

Von Herzen zu Herzen: may mean 'from one heart to another', or 'first to one heart, then to another'. *fliehen?*: some editors read 'Wie soll ich fliehen,'.

Written at Ilmenau near Weimar, May 1776. Goethe had been invited to
Weimar by the Duke of Weimar, Carl August, in 1775, and was to stay
there for almost the rest of his life. In this poem Goethe's restlessness and
prodigality in love are still apparent, although he had already met Charlotte
von Stein, who was soon to draw for a time all his love to herself.
The alternative to love is still a hermit-like seclusion in the woods
('wälderwärts ziehen'), to which Goethe, like Faust in the 'Wald und
Höhle' scene, still had recourse from time to time. But the poem is not
about such seclusion; its pounding beat is at one and the same time an
expression of ardour and of the jolting force of a love which is almost as
painful as suffering would be. (Yet the last lines do come, rhythmically, to
a softer close.)

AN DEN GEIST DES JOHANNES
SECUNDUS*

Lieber, heiliger, großer Küsser,
Der du mir's in lechzend atmender
Glückseligkeit fast vorgetan hast!
Wem soll ich's klagen, klag' ich dir's nicht!
Dir, dessen Lieder wie ein warmes Kissen
Heilender Kräuter mir unters Herz sich legten,
Daß es wieder aus dem krampfigen Starren
Erdetreibens* klopfend sich erholte.
Ach, wie klag' ich dir's, daß meine Lippe blutet,
Mir gespalten ist und erbärmlich schmerzet,
Meine Lippe, die so viel gewohnt ist
Von der Liebe süßtem Glück zu schwellen
Und, wie eine goldne Himmelspforte,
Lallende Seligkeit aus- und einzustammeln.
Gesprungen ist sie! Nicht vom Biß der Holden,
Die, in voller ringsumfangender Liebe,
Mehr möcht' haben von mir, und möchte mich Ganzen
Ganz erküssen, und fressen, und was sie könnte!
Nicht gesprungen, weil nach ihrem Hauche
Meine Lippen unheilige Lüfte* entweihten.
Ach, gesprungen, weil mich, öden, kalten,
Über beizenden Reif der Herbstwind anpackt.*

Und da ist Traubensaft und der Saft der Bienen,
An meines Herdes treuem Feuer vereinigt,
Der soll mir helfen! Wahrlich, er hilft nicht:
Denn von der Liebe alles heilendem
Gift-Balsam ist kein Tröpfchen drunter.

Johannes Secundus (1511–36) was a Netherlands poet whose collection of Latin poems, 'Basia' ('Kisses'), brought him European fame. *aus dem krampfigen Starren Erdetreibens*: 'out of the cramped rigidity of earth's daily round'. *unheilige Lüfte* is the subject of this sentence: the sense is really 'not because after kissing her my lips were desecrated by some other's kiss'. *weil mich...anpackt*: 'öden' and 'kalten' refer to 'mich' rather than to 'Reif' (hoar-frost).

LIEBEBEDÜRFNIS

Wer vernimmt mich? ach, wem soll ichs klagen?
Wers vernähme, würd er mich bedauern?
Ach, die Lippe, die so manche Freude
Sonst genossen hat und sonst gegeben,
Ist gespalten, und sie schmerzt erbärmlich.
Und sie ist nicht etwa wund geworden,
Weil die Liebste mich zu wild ergriffen,
Hold mich angebissen, daß sie fester
Sich des Freunds versichernd ihn genösse:
Nein, das zarte Lippchen ist gesprungen,
Weil nun über Reif und Frost die Winde
Spitz und scharf und lieblos mir begegnen.

Und nun soll mir Saft der edlen Traube,
Mit dem Saft der Bienen bei dem Feuer
Meines Herds vereinigt, Lindrung schaffen.
Ach, was will das helfen, mischt die Liebe
Nicht ein Tröpfchen ihres Balsams drunter?

The first of these poems was never published by Goethe: it is known to us only from one of his MSS dated 2 November 1776. The second, obviously a revision of the first, was published in 1789. Curiously, although Goethe was very shortly to publish the erotica of the *Römische Elegien*, this second version is prim by comparison with the original. Not only does the

regularization of the metre make it sound arch, there are turns of phrase which have a pedantic ring: 'sie ist *nicht etwa* wund geworden', 'daß sie... ihn *genösse*'—and also some preciosity ('das zarte Lippchen') and some alarming attempts at preserving the decencies ('Weil die Liebste...*hold mich angebissen*'—and the substitution of 'Balsam' for 'Gift-Balsam'). The frank freshness of the original, its rhythmic sincerity and sometimes boisterous humour have given place to a coy, self-conscious piece of classicizing. One becomes aware that in some ways Goethe had taken a turn for the worse in his first Weimar years, and that even the Italian Journey of 1786–8, with all its liberating effects, had not yet fully brought home to him the falsity, since he could still in 1789 prefer to publish the second of these poems rather than the first.

Warum gabst du* uns die tiefen Blicke,
Unsre Zukunft ahndungsvoll* zu schaun,
Unsrer Liebe, unserm Erdenglücke
Wähnend selig* nimmer hinzutraun?
Warum gabst uns, Schicksal, die Gefühle,
Uns einander in das Herz zu sehn,
Um durch all die seltenen Gewühle
Unser wahr Verhältnis auszuspähn?

Ach, so viele tausend Menschen kennen,
Dumpf sich treibend, kaum ihr eigen Herz,
Schweben zwecklos hin und her und rennen
Hoffnungslos in unversehnem Schmerz;
Jauchzen wieder, wenn der schnellen Freuden
Unerwart'te Morgenröte tagt.
Nur uns armen liebevollen beiden
Ist das wechselseitige Glück versagt,
Uns zu lieben, ohn uns zu verstehen,
In dem andern sehn, was er nie war,
Immer frisch auf Traumglück auszugehen
Und zu schwanken auch in Traumgefahr.

Glücklich, den ein leerer Traum beschäftigt!
Glücklich, dem die Ahndung eitel wär!
Jede Gegenwart und jeder Blick bekräftigt

Traum und Ahndung leider uns noch mehr.
Sag, was will das Schicksal uns bereiten?
Sag, wie band es uns so rein genau?
Ach, du warst in abgelebten Zeiten*
Meine Schwester oder meine Frau.

Kanntest jeden Zug in meinem Wesen,
Spähtest, wie die reinste Nerve klingt,
Konntest mich mit Einem Blicke* lesen,
Den so schwer ein sterblich Aug durchdringt;
Tropftest Mäßigung dem heißen Blute,
Richtetest den wilden irren Lauf,
Und in deinen Engelsarmen ruhte
Die zerstörte Brust sich wieder auf;
Hieltest zauberleicht ihn angebunden
Und vergaukeltest* ihm manchen Tag.
Welche Seligkeit glich jenen Wonnestunden,
Da er dankbar dir zu Füßen lag,
Fühlt' sein Herz an deinem Herzen schwellen,
Fühlte sich in deinem Auge gut,
Alle seine Sinnen sich erhellen
Und beruhigen sein brausend Blut!

Und von allem dem schwebt ein Erinnern
Nur noch um das ungewisse Herz,
Fühlt die alte Wahrheit ewig gleich im Innern,
Und der neue Zustand wird ihm Schmerz.
Und wir scheinen uns nur halb beseelet,
Dämmernd ist um uns der hellste Tag.
Glücklich, daß das Schicksal, das uns quälet,
Uns doch nicht verändern mag!*

Warum gabst du: the 'du' refers to Destiny, as appears in line 5. *ahndungsvoll*: 'Ahndung', or in modern German 'Ahnung', means intuition, in this case with a certain sense of foreboding. *wähnend selig*: 'imagining it (our love, our earthly happiness) to be blissful (even if it is not so)'. The general sense of these lines is: 'Why, Destiny, will you never allow us to trust in this present love we feel, imagining that to be true bliss, instead of reminding us continually of our far deeper love, beyond this mere present?' *abgelebten Zeiten*: times already lived through (in former existences, presumably). *mit Einem Blicke*: the capital 'E' is here a form of emphasis. *vergaukeltest*: 'you charmed away'. *mag*: 'vermag'.

Written as a letter to Charlotte von Stein ('Lida', as she became known to the public), the wife of a court official at Weimar, and sent on 14 April 1776, that is, a few months after Goethe had first met her and well before he had settled down to Weimar life. Goethe kept no copy and did not publish the verses himself; they have, however, become extremely well known, especially the last two lines of the third stanza.

Superficial reading of the poem has established the impression (challenged by Emil Staiger) that it is a tribute to Charlotte's healing influence on Goethe at Weimar. In reality it is something more subtle and revealing. Goethe is groping his way into this experience: the opening lines are difficult for that very reason, although their tone is calm. It is as though he were talking to himself—he knows, as we do not, that it is Fate he is addressing, or perhaps not even he is quite aware of what his first question means till he has put it. The sense, as it gradually crystallizes, is that this love of theirs is different from that of other mortals, who are only too glad to be deceived. Others like to be blinded by love into accepting their lover as the ideal perfection; he and Charlotte cannot enjoy this happiness, such as it is (though there are moments when it seems to him even desirable to be so deluded). They are compelled to see each other as they really are, falling far short of the ideal, and this is so painful that Goethe begins by asking Fate why it has played him so unkind a turn.

In an undated letter to Charlotte, which seems to have been written at about this time, Goethe writes: 'Wir können einander nichts sein und sind einander zu viel...eben weil ich die Sachen nur seh', wie sie sind—das macht mich rasend.' He and she could be 'nothing' to each other because Charlotte was married, and had no intention of leaving her husband. They were 'too much' to each other in a different sense, which the second half of the poem brings out. From the line 'Sag, was will das Schicksal uns bereiten' onwards, Goethe speaks to Charlotte in tones of complete confidence and trust in her ability to understand—there is something moving about the simplicity of his language and the throwaway 'Ach' with which he tells her that there must be some metaphysical bond between them. However, what he tells her is not that she is now healing him as a sister heals a brother—all that calm he speaks of was in a former existence, and there is nothing left of it now but 'ein Erinnern'. He knows somehow that it was so once, but it is not so now, and his heart is uncertain (as it was once with Friederike—'Ob ich dich liebe, weiß ich nicht'—?). Goethe has the frankness to tell Charlotte that his present condition is painful, his life miserable even though he loves her, in comparison with his intuitive awareness of that former existence. His only solace, in the last two lines of all, is that Fate may torment them and yet not change that everlasting mutual bond (or so one may understand the reference to 'verändern'.)

The strange detachment in Goethe (p. 3 above), whereby he was so seldom wholly involved in love, thus takes a new turn. Seeing quite

frankly that he does not admire Charlotte in the way lovers are supposed to do, Goethe perceives that his feelings for her can only be accounted for in relation to that metaphysical realm where detachment from mortal feelings is proper. The Maxim of La Rochefoucauld (no. 69) seems relevant here: 'If there exists a love which is pure and free from any admixture of other passions, it is so buried in the depths of our hearts that we are unaware of its existence.' Yet perhaps Goethe's frank, steady-paced, almost tidally flowing and ebbing verse conveys as much of it as anyone can be aware of.

LIEBHABER IN ALLEN GESTALTEN

Ich wollt, ich wär ein Fisch,
So hurtig und frisch;
Und kämst du zu anglen,
Ich würde nicht manglen.
Ich wollt, ich wär ein Fisch,
So hurtig und frisch.

Ich wollt, ich wär ein Pferd,
Da wär ich dir wert.
O wär ich ein Wagen,
Bequem dich zu tragen.
Ich wollt, ich wär ein Pferd,
Da wär ich dir wert.

Ich wollt, ich wäre Gold,
Dir immer im Sold;
Und tätst du was kaufen,
Käm ich wieder gelaufen.
Ich wollt, ich wäre Gold,
Dir immer im Sold.

Ich wollt, ich wär treu,
Mein Liebchen stets neu;
Ich wollt mich verheißen,*
Wollt nimmer verreisen.
Ich wollt, ich wär treu,
Mein Liebchen stets neu.

Ich wollt, ich wär alt
Und runzlig und kalt;
Tätst du mirs versagen,
Da könnt mich nichts plagen,
Ich wollt, ich wär alt
Und runzlig und kalt.

Wär ich Affe sogleich
Voll neckender Streich;
Hätt was dich verdrossen,
So macht ich dir Possen.
Wär ich Affe sogleich
Voll neckender Streich.

Wär ich gut wie ein Schaf,
Wie der Löwe so brav;
Hätt Augen wie's Lüchschen
Und Listen wie's Füchschen.
Wär ich gut wie ein Schaf,
Wie der Löwe so brav.

Was alles ich wär,
Das gönnt ich dir sehr;
Mit fürstlichen Gaben,
Du solltest mich haben.
Was alles ich wär,
Das gönnt ich dir sehr.

Doch bin ich, wie ich bin,
Und nimm mich nur hin!
Willst du Beßre besitzen,
So laß sie dir schnitzen.
Ich bin nun, wie ich bin;
So nimm mich nur hin!

mich verheißen: 'bind myself by vows'.

Exact date not known, probably before 1780.

WOODS AND
LAKES

WOODS AND LAKES

In seventeenth-century Germany the fields seem to have been places to work in or fight over or travel through. Poets, at all events, used natural scenes seldom, or only by way of adornment or allegory. (Presumably people enjoyed the country all the same—they did in Holland, to judge by the landscape painting of that time.) It is not until the eighteenth century that, as in the poem *Die Alpen* by the Swiss Albrecht von Haller, and in Klopstock's poem on Lake Zürich, descriptions of Nature become interesting or moving in their own right. And even with Klopstock the effect is curiously subdued, the colours 'röt*lich*' rather than plain 'rot', as though the civilized eye could not see the full splendour of things.

Goethe was one of the first in his generation to recognize that a landscape is a mood. The pressure of the bud against its outer casing was his own gaiety breaking forth, and the diffused light of the moon was his own peaceful frame of mind—these were not similes or metaphors, so he felt, but living counterparts of his own condition. So powerful was this conviction that he even turned to scientific examination of flowers, clouds and rocks, trying to demonstrate that there was an inward life in them closely mirroring his own. Everything was part of one great unity which he thought to have been described in the philosophical works of Spinoza. It was not so much pantheism as what has inelegantly been called 'panenhenism' (from the Greek 'pan' and 'hen', 'all' and 'one'—'all-in-one-ism'): a unity in which the pattern of the whole was reiterated in the pattern of all the individual parts, as the solar system is reiterated in the structure of an atom.

That, at least, was the outcome of Goethe's search by the time he left for Italy, in 1786, when for a while he imagined himself to be in the possession of the 'key to all the realms of Nature'. Its result in poetry was so little pleasing a work as the 'Metamorphose der Pflanzen'. The instinctive feeling of

kinship, on the other hand, remained all through his life, and inspired some of Goethe's best poetry. He did not always find consolation in Nature: sometimes, as for Werther, she was for him the symbol of the senseless destruction, re-creation and destruction of the world's processes—'Geburt und Grab, ein ewiges Meer'. By and large, however, Goethe saw those processes as healing and healthful, and almost all his nature-poetry reflects that view.

<div style="text-align:center">* * *</div>

MAILIED

Wie herrlich leuchtet
Mir die Natur!
Wie glänzt die Sonne!
Wie lacht die Flur!

Es dringen Blüten
Aus jedem Zweig
Und tausend Stimmen
Aus dem Gesträuch

Und Freud und Wonne
Aus jeder Brust.
O Erd, o Sonne,
O Glück, o Lust,

O Lieb, o Liebe,
So golden schön,
Wie Morgenwolken
Auf jenen Höhn,

Du segnest herrlich
Das frische Feld—
Im Blütendampfe
Die volle Welt!

O Mädchen, Mädchen,
Wie lieb ich dich!
Wie blickt dein Auge,*
Wie liebst du mich!

So liebt die Lerche
Gesang und Luft,
Und Morgenblumen
Den Himmelsduft,

Wie ich dich liebe
Mit warmem Blut,
Die du mir Jugend
Und Freud und Mut

Zu neuen Liedern
Und Tänzen gibst.
Sei ewig glücklich,
Wie du mich liebst!*

Wie blickt dein Auge: this is probably a misprint for *blinkt*, but the word was never corrected in the editions which appeared in Goethe's lifetime. *Wie du mich liebst*: the sense is not very definite: 'be eternally happy, because that is just what you are when you love me'—something like that, perhaps.

Written in May 1771, originally with the title 'Maifest', and meant for Friederike Brion, this is outstanding among the 'Sesenheimer Lieder', above all for its mounting ecstasy. In the present version the original punctuation is preserved, substituting commas for the exclamation marks which were inserted in later editions. This brings home the strong impetus which carries the thought and emotion through from one verse to another. Just as 'dringen' in the first line of verse 2 is made to go on serving the nouns of verse 3, fusing blossoms and birdsongs and human emotions, so the idea which begins at 'O Erd, o Sonne' carries on to the end of verse 5. The next verse marks a more static moment before the long phrase of mounting excitement sets in at 'So liebt die Lerche', to end only just before the quieter couplet that rounds it all off. These telling rhythms contrast well with those of 'Balde seh ich Rickchen wieder' (p. 9 above). Apart from that, the poem has distinctive words: 'dringen' calls for our attention; so do the 'Morgenwolken'; and the blessing of love that is conveyed in a 'Blüten*dampf*'. 'Die *volle* Welt' is also unusual in sense and feeling: 'die ganze Welt' would have been less striking.

AUS DEM TAGEBUCH DER REISE
IN DIE SCHWEIZ

Ich saug' an meiner Nabelschnur*
Nun Nahrung aus der Welt.
Und herrlich rings ist die Natur,
Die mich am Busen hält.
Die Welle wieget unsern Kahn
Im Rudertakt hinauf,
Und Berge Wolken angetan
Entgegnen* unserm Lauf.

Aug mein Aug, was sinkst du nieder?
Goldne Träume, kommt ihr wieder?
Weg, du Traum, so gold du bist,
Hier auch Lieb und Leben ist.
Auf der Welle blinken
Tausend schwebende Sterne,
Liebe Nebel trinken
Rings die türmende Ferne,
Morgenwind umflügelt
Die beschattete Bucht,
Und im See bespiegelt
Sich die reifende Frucht.

Nabelschnur: 'umbilical cord'. *entgegnen*: 'begegnen', 'to meet' (nowadays 'to reply').

Written in Goethe's diary under the heading '15. Junius 1775, aufm Zürichersee', followed by another heading, 'Vom Berge in die See. Vid. das Privat Archiv des Dichters. Lit. L.' and the poem given on p. 13 above. 'See Poet's Private Archives, Letter L.' is a reference to Lili Schönemann, whom Goethe was seeking to evade by travelling to Switzerland (see p. xv above).

The poem is another impromptu piece, which Goethe corrected before publishing it as 'Auf dem See' in 1789. The humorous extravagance of the first two lines, with its very literal picture of the 'child of Nature', was amended, and in general the affectionate tone was muted. The mountains, here said to be 'attached' to the clouds (in the emotional sense, as one says 'ich bin ihm angetan') became 'Berge, wolkig himmelan'. The '*liebe*

32

Nebel' became 'weiche Nebel'. But the sense of things meeting and joining together remained—the Alps still came towards the boat, the stars in the sky were still rocking on the waters of the lake, the towering heights were drunk up by the mists. And this was what mattered. Goethe had escaped from Lili, to whom he had just become engaged, and though the dream of her recurred to him he was able to say 'Hier auch Lieb und Leben ist'— not that he had fallen in love with someone else, but there was 'love' in the natural scene which he had been about to give up for her sake. The poem thus becomes a symbol of the solitary fulfilment in woods and fields which was always Goethe's alternative to the love of women.

The changes in rhythm, from the lounging ease of the first verse to the drowsiness of the first two lines of the second, and the sudden liveliness of the last ten lines, reflect Goethe's moods.

IM HERBST 1775

Fetter grüne,* du Laub,
Das Rebengeländer,
Hier mein Fenster herauf.*
Gedrängter quillet,*
Zwillingsbeeren, und reifet
Schneller und glänzend voller.

Euch brütet der Mutter Sonne
Scheideblick, euch umsäuselt
Des holden Himmels
Fruchtende Fülle.
Euch kühlet des Monds
Freundlicher Zauberhauch,
Und euch betauen, ach,
Aus diesen Augen
Der ewig belebenden Liebe
Voll schwellende Tränen.

Fetter grüne: 'grow green more lushly'. *herauf*: by ellipsis, the sentence means 'grow up the vine-trellis by my window'. *Gedrängter quillet*: 'swell (and swirl with sap) more tautly (or closer together)'. Later versions read 'quellet'.

Written in 1775 before Goethe finally left Lili Schönemann. Published in 1789 as 'Herbstgefühl'. More incisive than any of Goethe's youthful

poetry, both in the upthrust of the rhythm and in the words that convey the taut juiciness of the grapes (Zwillingsbeeren—no commentator seems to have found a really satisfying explanation of their being 'twinned'). The emotion is strangely poised between enjoyment of the sheer fleshy vitality of the vine, awareness of transience (perhaps—is the 'Scheideblick' the sun's parting glance before plunging into winter?) and the sense that this vitality is intimately close to his own overflowing tears of love ('voll schwellend' seems meant to recall the grapes again). Goethe enters the life of the vine here not only with the feel of the words in the mouth but in ways almost imperceptible. At the same time, he is one with all the great loving powers that tend its life from outside.

The poem gains in meaning through association with 'Wonne der Wehmut', where again the living quality of things is linked with tears. But the latter poem *states* an idea, whereas 'Im Herbst' embodies one.

WONNE DER WEHMUT

Trocknet nicht, trocknet nicht,
Tränen der heiligen Liebe!
Ach, den halbtrocknen Augen schon
Wie öde, tot ist die Welt!
Trocknet nicht, trocknet nicht,
Tränen der ewigen Liebe!

Written in 1775. These are not the words set by Beethoven, but are from a copy by Herder, not printed in Goethe's lifetime. The sense of ll. 3–4 is that eyes which have so much as begun to cease weeping will see the world as deserted and dead. Compare the preceding poem.

AN DEN MOND

Füllest wieder Busch und Tal
Still mit Nebelglanz,
Lösest endlich auch einmal
Meine Seele ganz;

Breitest über mein Gefild
Lindernd deinen Blick,

Wie des Freundes Auge mild
Über mein Geschick.

Jeden Nachklang fühlt mein Herz
Froh- und trüber Zeit,
Wandle zwischen Freud und Schmerz
In der Einsamkeit.

Fließe, fließe, lieber Fluß!
Nimmer werd ich froh,
So verrauschte Scherz und Kuß,
Und die Treue so.

Ich besaß es doch einmal,
Was so köstlich ist!
Daß man doch zu seiner Qual
Nimmer es vergißt!

Rausche, Fluß, das Tal entlang,
Ohne Rast und Ruh,
Rausche, flüstre meinem Sang
Melodien zu,

Wenn du in der Winternacht
Wütend überschwillst,
Oder um die Frühlingspracht
Junger Knospen quillst.

Selig, wer sich vor der Welt
Ohne Haß verschließt,
Einen Freund am Busen hält
Und mit dem genießt,

Was, von Menschen nicht gewußt
Oder nicht bedacht,
Durch das Labyrinth der Brust
Wandelt in der Nacht.

A first version was written between 1776 and 1778, and seemed to refer to Charlotte von Stein (in verse 2 'des Freundes Auge' then read 'der Liebsten Auge'). The present version is that published in 1789, possibly revised in the light of suggestions from Charlotte, certainly after Goethe had broken with her. The idea that the poem was occasioned by the suicide of Christine Lassberg in the river Ilm no longer seems probable: it is now thought to have been begun earlier.

The movement of the verse begins dreamily, in harmony with the vague, floating sensation inspired by the moonlight, and at first the poet is at peace, his soul 'gelöst'—dissolved as it were in the gleaming mists. He is 're-collected', the past being fully present to him, and in this strange moment outside normal time he feels '*zwischen* Freud und Schmerz'. A letter to Charlotte of about this time (16 September 1776) speaks of a state of mind seemingly like this one: 'Ich bin in einem unendlich reinen Mittelzustand ohne Freud und Schmerz, zusammengepackt von Tausenderley Um-ständen ohne gedrängt zu seyn.' In the version of 'Der du von dem Him-mel bist' written in the same year he speaks just as strangely of Peace as that which 'Alle Freud und Schmerzen stillest' (the later version removes the surprise by changing this to 'Alles *Leid* und Schmerzen'). The significance of the line in 'An den Mond' may thus be one of well-nigh mystical detach-ment from passions of all kinds—'between' in the sense of being attached to neither.

With the fourth verse, however, the calm movement changes to an almost desperate cry—whatever the former state may have been, the sight of the flowing river recalls the transience of things, and at the same time the unforgettable delight (has it perhaps to do with that eternal bond Goethe speaks of in 'Warum gabst du uns die tiefen Blicke'?) which he no longer enjoys. He is a spirit in Time, and the moonlight rather reminds him of what he has lost than restores it to him.

At once, the poem begins to work towards a resolution: like the river, the poet is *in* Time and must flow along with it. Let him then sweep restlessly forward, and let the onward movement be the inspiration of his poetry whether in the fearful melodies of winter or the lovelier ones of Spring. All life, all contrasts, without distinction, are his theme, as they are for Faust. If detachment in an all-inclusive moment will not serve, he will embrace all human experience, 'was der ganzen Menschheit zugeteilt ist', as *Faust* has it.

Yet this is not *the* resolution. Strangely, the poem does not end here, or on some extension of the same idea, but reverts in the last two verses to a thought which had been present from the poem's inception. The attempted solution through the river-image had not been in the earliest version, which lacked the central verses, but the strong assertion at the end, that bliss was to be had only apart from the world, was always there. Now, in the final version, the two solutions stand side by side, without a trace of linkage.

What do the last two verses mean? It seems likely that they refer back to the title, for the moon, to whom the poem is addressed, can hardly have disappeared from thought completely after verse 2. Frau von Stein certainly thought that the 'Was' of verse 9 meant the moon, for the last lines in her own re-writing of the poem read 'In dem himmlischen Gewand | glänzet bei der Nacht'. Goethe's meaning was more complex than that, since he speaks of a movement through the 'Labyrinth der Brust'. But he was acquainted with the mystical idea of an indwelling *sun* as a source of vitality; in *Wilhelm Meister* he uses a similar notion in describing the saintly woman Makarie, and in the present poem, cryptic though it is, he may have meant to hint at a source of peace both within and outside the human heart.

Whether Goethe meant to oppose the detachment of the last two verses to the universal embrace implied by the preceding two cannot be guessed from this poem. In later years he decidedly did think it desirable to reconcile both these attitudes (see the aphorisms on p. 187 below). Looking back from our knowledge of his later poetry, one sees a bare suggestion of the idea of polarity (see p. 49).

WANDRERS NACHTLIED

Über allen Gipfeln
Ist Ruh,
In allen Wipfeln
Spürest du
Kaum einen Hauch;
Die Vögelein schweigen im Walde.
Warte nur, balde
Ruhest du auch.

Usually printed immediately after the other 'Wandrers Nachtlied' (p. 115 below), to whose plea for peace it is like a reply, and with the title 'Ein Gleiches', i.e. another 'Wandrers Nachtlied'. Goethe often spoke of himself as 'der Wandrer', especially in poems. This one was written on the wall of the wooden hunting-cabin on the Gickelhahn hill by Ilmenau, where Goethe often spent the night; the date was 6 September 1780. Here again he was 'zwischen Freud und Schmerz'.

Schubert's setting is very well known.

MEERES STILLE

Tiefe Stille herrscht im Wasser,
Ohne Regung ruht das Meer,
Und bekümmert sieht der Schiffer
Glatte Fläche ringsumher.
Keine Luft von keiner Seite!
Todesstille fürchterlich!
In der ungeheuern Weite
Reget keine Welle sich.

GLÜCKLICHE FAHRT

Die Nebel zerreißen,
Der Himmel ist helle,
Und Äolus* löset
Das ängstliche Band.
Es säuseln die Winde,
Es rührt sich der Schiffer.
Geschwinde! Geschwinde!
Es teilt sich die Welle,
Es naht sich die Ferne;
Schon seh ich das Land!

Aeolus the god held the winds in a sack; the untying of 'das ängstliche Band' ('ängstlich' is a transferred epithet) released them.

These two poems, always printed together, were written in 1795 or perhaps earlier. They might almost be meant to display the contrasting effects of trochaic and dactylic feet, although it is probable, at this period of his life, that Goethe was seeking to convey the 'Idea' of stillness and that of movement. The poems contrast in subtlety with the nature-lyrics of the time before the Italian Journey.

GENIUS OR
DEMI-GOD

GENIUS OR DEMI-GOD

'Bin ich ein Gott? Mir wird so licht!' The words are Faust's, but the temptation to utter them must have been Goethe's at times. The view of the poet he received from Herder at Strasbourg in 1771 regarded him—or at least regarded Shakespeare—as a Creator who fashioned a whole world of living beings out of his own soul. He was a many-faceted being, volcanic in his fury, responsible to none in his superabundant vitality. Yet like the myriad constituents of a Gothic cathedral, all his creations formed one whole, 'alles zweckend zum Ganzen'. And perhaps Shakespeare did know the temptation to feel that apotheosis too. Hamlet could be bounded in a nutshell and yet count himself king of infinite space, 'were it not that I have bad dreams'. Lear, in his madness, complains that he has been deceived: 'They told me I was every thing.' Goethe, trying to follow in Shakespeare's steps, and with Spinoza's pantheism to colour his view, was perhaps more prone to see his own creativity in this light. If he could feel the natural world of buds and grass, sun and moon, as in some way within him, might he not be at the least, and as Faust said, an 'Ebenbild der Gottheit'?

Herder's teaching was concerned with the poet as dramatist, as the man who lives imaginatively in scores of different characters and is not necessarily committed to the views or the identity of any one of them. It was peculiarly suited to the 'chamaeleon' Goethe, with his detachment from his own emotions even when deeply in love, and his ability to feel himself both in and out of a situation at one and the same time. And thus Goethe's Titanism, the very impulse to dethrone the gods and put himself in their place, could become a dramatic monologue in the person of some character which he assumed for a while only. It is not so surprising that he wrote the iconoclastic 'Prometheus' and the adoring 'Ganymed' both within the same year, for they were not

necessarily confessions of personal belief or disbelief, but could be masks briefly adopted.

Yet Goethe was not always a dramatist and not always concerned with writing dramatic monologues. There are poems in which he surely speaks with his own voice, and others in which it may not have occurred to him to make any clear distinction. In 'Harzreise im Winter', the poem in which he ultimately appears more godlike than in any other, his identity flits briefly over several figures, yet one cannot say he is really detached. In 'An Schwager Kronos', decidedly a humorous poem, he is more than half committed to his fantasy.

The grandiose temptations come to an end, however, shortly after Goethe's arrival at Weimar in 1775. By the early 1780's that adaptability which had stood him in such good stead hitherto had led him into accepting a life which he was very soon to find intolerable. The poems in which he records that acceptance, 'Ilmenau' and 'Zueignung', bear the marks of the strain he was now forced to feel.

* * *

MAHOMETS-GESANG

Seht den Felsenquell,
Freudehell,
Wie ein Sternenblick!*
Über Wolken
Nährten seine Jugend
Gute Geister
Zwischen Klippen im Gebüsch.

Jünglingsfrisch
Tanzt er aus der Wolke
Auf die Marmorfelsen nieder,
Jauchzet wieder
Nach dem Himmel.

Durch die Gipfelgänge
Jagt er bunten Kieseln nach,
Und mit frühem Führertritt
Reißt er seine Bruderquellen
Mit sich fort.

Drunten werden in dem Tal
Unter seinem Fußtritt Blumen,
Und die Wiese
Lebt von seinem Hauch.

Doch ihn hält kein Schattental,
Keine Blumen,
Die ihm seine Knie umschlingen,
Ihm mit Liebesaugen schmeicheln;
Nach der Ebne dringt sein Lauf,
Schlangewandelnd.

Bäche schmiegen
Sich gesellig an.
Nun tritt er
In die Ebne silberprangend,
Und die Ebne prangt mit ihm,
Und die Flüsse von der Ebne
Und die Bäche von Gebürgen
Jauchzen ihm und rufen: Bruder,
Bruder, nimm die Brüder mit,
Mit, zu deinem alten Vater,
Zu dem ew'gen Ozean,
Der mit weitverbreit'ten Armen
Unsrer wartet;*
Die sich, ach, vergebens öffnen,
Seine Sehnenden zu fassen;
Denn uns frißt in öder Wüste
Gier'ger Sand,
Die Sonne droben
Saugt an unserm Blut.

Ein Hügel
Hemmet uns zum Teiche.
Bruder,
Nimm die Brüder von der Ebne,
Nimm die Brüder von Gebürgen
Mit, zu deinem Vater mit!

Kommt ihr alle! —
Und nun schwillt er
Herrlicher, ein ganz Geschlechte
Trägt den Fürsten hoch empor,
Und im rollenden Triumphe
Gibt er Ländern Namen, Städte
Werden unter seinem Fuß.

Unaufhaltsam rauscht er über,
Läßt der Türne* Flammengipfel,
Marmorhäuser, eine Schöpfung
Seiner Fülle, hinter sich.

Zedernhäuser* trägt der Atlas
Auf den Riesenschultern, sausend
Wehen über seinem Haupte
Tausend Segel auf zum Himmel
Seine Macht und Herrlichkeit.

Und so trägt er seine Brüder,
Seine Schätze, seine Kinder
Dem erwartenden Erzeuger
Freudebrausend an das Herz.

Sternenblick: 'blick' here in the sense of 'glint'. *Unsrer wartet*: 'waits for us'. *Türne*: 'Türme'. *Zedernhäuser*: i.e. ships.

Written in the winter 1772–3, this was originally meant to form part of a play, *Mahomet*, and was divided into speeches by Fatema and Ali. It is thus a 'Mahomets-Gesang' in the sense that it is about Mahomet, not that it is sung by him. (The hyphen is important.)

This is not, then, a direct personal expression of Goethe's 'philosophy'. In this personification of the river as a man completing the cycle of his life,

44

Goethe does convey an exultant, life-affirming mood quite opposed to the conventional view of religion in his time, where the emphasis lay all on repentance for sin and the expectation of joy in a life to come. It appears from his account in *Dichtung und Wahrheit* (book 14), however, that in the context of the whole play the 'Gesang' would have had its meaning modified. It was to have been sung at the height of Mahomet's success, but in achieving this success the prophet would have been obliged to sully the purity of his heavenly message, as Goethe believed was inevitable with all who sought to translate heaven to earth. Shortly after, the prophet was to have been poisoned by a vengeful woman, and to have made a deathbed repentance: 'er reinigt seine Lehre, befestigt sein Reich und stirbt', says Goethe. The triumph of the song, in which no hint of the prophet's imperfection appears, must then have been modified by the ending. Still, it is significant that only the song and one other fragment were ever written—one sees where Goethe's first thoughts lay, and indeed the poem is a forecast of his own life.

The personification is at times pure allegory, with the pebbles representing childish games, the flowers sweethearts, the streams disciples or friends. The image is not always quite appropriate—it is not apparent how the main stream enables the tributaries to flow over the hills and sandbanks that obstruct them. On the other hand there is such pleasing imagery as that of the meadows living by the 'breath' of the stream. But the poem is more concerned with creating the sense of a mighty progress than with exploring the complexities inherent in it, and rhythmically it is most successful. The short lines of the beginning (perhaps inviting a breathed mystery in the voice) gradually give way to a measure, a trochaic tetrameter, which first appears at line 10, then recurs singly once or twice, then in twos and threes. After 'In die Ebne silberprangend' the same metre recurs eight times in twelve lines although at 'Gier'ger Sand' it is reduced to the parched voice of the streams in the desert. Thereafter, at 'Nimm die Brüder...', the metre establishes itself completely, with a marching tread as triumphant as that of the river.

The poem invites comparison with Hölderlin's 'Der Rhein', or his easier 'Heidelberg', in both of which the river serves as an image of human life.

PROMETHEUS

Bedecke deinen Himmel, Zeus,
Mit Wolkendunst!
Und übe, Knaben* gleich,
Der Disteln köpft,
An Eichen dich und Bergeshöhn!

Mußt mir meine Erde
Doch lassen stehn,
Und meine Hütte,
Die du nicht gebaut,
Und meinen Herd,
Um dessen Glut
Du mich beneidest.

Ich kenne nichts Ärmer's
Unter der Sonn' als euch Götter.
Ihr nähret kümmerlich
Von Opfersteuern
Und Gebetshauch
Eure Majestät
Und darbtet, wären
Nicht Kinder und Bettler
Hoffnungsvolle Toren.

Da ich ein Kind war,
Nicht wußte, wo aus, wo ein,
Kehrte mein verirrtes Aug'
Zur Sonne, als wenn drüber wär'
Ein Ohr, zu hören meine Klage,
Ein Herz wie meins,
Sich des Bedrängten zu erbarmen.

Wer half mir
Wider der Titanen* Übermut?
Wer rettete vom Tode mich,
Von Sklaverei?
Hast du's nicht alles selbst vollendet,
Heilig glühend Herz?
Und glühtest, jung und gut,
Betrogen, Rettungsdank
Dem Schlafenden dadroben?

Ich dich ehren? Wofür?
Hast du die Schmerzen gelindert

Je des Beladenen?
Hast du die Tränen gestillet
Je des Geängsteten?

Hat nicht mich zum Manne geschmiedet
Die allmächtige Zeit
Und das ewige Schicksal,
Meine Herrn und deine?

Wähntest du etwa,
Ich sollte das Leben hassen,
In Wüsten fliehn,
Weil nicht alle Knabenmorgen-
Blütenträume reiften?

Hier sitz' ich, forme Menschen
Nach meinem Bilde,
Ein Geschlecht, das mir gleich sei,
Zu leiden, weinen,
Genießen und zu freuen sich,
Und dein nicht zu achten,
Wie ich.

Knaben: understand 'dem Knaben'. *Titanen*: the Titans were giants or gods who overthrew the ruling gods, in Greek mythology.

Written in the autumn of 1774, this (an early version) is in some ways a dramatic monologue. Goethe planned a play on Prometheus of which this poem was *not* a part, although inevitably the hero would have expressed similar defiance of the gods. As in *Mahomet*, however, it appears that the proud self-assertion would have been countered to some extent in the context of the whole. How little of a personal utterance the poem was may be seen from Goethe's annoyance when Jacobi published it in 1785 without his permission. Even though it appeared anonymously, Goethe feared that it would be recognized as his and taken as an expression of unbelief on his own account. (See also *Dichtung und Wahrheit*, book 15.)

On the other hand, there are passages inappropriate to Prometheus, and more appropriate to Goethe, which do suggest his personal involvement. The Prometheus of Greek myth was punished for his theft of fire from heaven by Zeus, who condemned him to be bound to a rock where a vulture consumed his liver interminably. He was rescued from this living

death not by his own powers but by Hercules. Goethe, however, in the lines beginning 'Wer rettete vom Tode mich', suggests that Prometheus accomplished his own release, and even that he was deluded into thanking Zeus for it. This must surely refer to some metaphorical death and slavery to which Goethe had felt himself subject—something of his rejection of a Christian upbringing has gone into these lines. It is in fact rather strange, though to a certain extent typical of Goethe (who said of himself that he was by nature incapable of writing a tragedy), that so little hint of Prometheus' terrible torments is given, and that his release is taken for granted as something already accomplished. Like the 'Mahomets-Gesang', the 'Prometheus' poem for all its vigour has only one mood: it does not explore the implications of human revolt.

The poem is in the main a straightforward piece of defiance, but not without some subtlety of tone in the original version printed here. A certain aloofness, incompatible with furious indignation (such as can be heard in the recording by the Deutsche Grammophongesellschaft 43 008 LPMS), is noticeable from time to time. True, the 'übe' in line 3 gives a contemptuous spurt of breath, untranslatable since the glottal stop has no such force in English, which might establish a harsher mood. But the image of the boy chopping thistles at once makes Zeus look ridiculous and relaxes tension, and thereafter the tone is too confident for fury. The last two words suggest an indifferent turning away, rather than a chest-beating confrontation.

GANYMED

Wie im Morgenglanze
Du rings mich anglühst,
Frühling, Geliebter!
Mit tausendfacher Liebeswonne
Sich an mein Herz drängt
Deiner ewigen Wärme
Heilig Gefühl,
Unendliche Schöne!

Daß ich dich fassen möcht
In diesen Arm!

Ach, an deinem Busen
Lieg ich, schmachte,
Und deine Blumen, dein Gras

Drängen sich an mein Herz.
Du kühlst den brennenden
Durst meines Busens,
Lieblicher Morgenwind!
Ruft drein die Nachtigall
Liebend nach mir aus dem Nebeltal.

Ich komm, ich komme!
Wohin? Ach, wohin?

Hinauf! Hinauf strebts.
Es schweben die Wolken
Abwärts, die Wolken
Neigen sich der sehnenden Liebe.
Mir! Mir!
In euerm Schoße
Aufwärts!
Umfangend umfangen!
Aufwärts an deinen Busen,
Allliebender Vater!

Probably written in the spring of 1774. The mood here is the precise
opposite of that in 'Prometheus', for Ganymede was the beautiful boy
whom Zeus loved and raised up to Olympus to be his cup-bearer.
The intensity of the rhythms is like that of 'Im Herbst 1775', not at all
like Schubert's setting. As in the poem on Lake Zürich (p. 32), there is
everywhere a movement of things towards one another.

Taken together with 'Prometheus' this poem is one of the first clear-cut
examples of Goethe's doctrine of 'Polarity', later more consciously cultivated
—the idea that 'polar' opposites (like the poles of a magnet) are complemen-
tary to one another, and that the highest wisdom is to realize all such
opposites (good and evil, hatred and love, rejection and acceptance, male
and female) in oneself. This doctrine, which has close affinities in Taoism, is
reflected in 'An den Mond', as has been seen. It recurs in 'Harzreise im
Winter' and elsewhere, although not always obviously (see especially pp. 59,
71, 152, 159, 164, 177, 181, 183, 186, 188 below).

ADLER UND TAUBE

Ein Adlersjüngling hob die Flügel
Nach Raub aus;
Ihn traf des Jägers Pfeil und schnitt
Der rechten Schwinge Sennkraft* ab.
Er stürzt' hinab in einen Myrtenhain,
Fraß seinen Schmerz drei Tage lang,
Und zuckt' an Qual
Drei lange, lange Nächte lang;
Zuletzt heilt' ihn
Allgegenwärtger Balsam
Allheilender Natur.
Er schleicht aus dem Gebüsch hervor
Und reckt die Flügel — ach!
Die Schwingkraft weggeschnitten —
Hebt sich mühsam kaum
Am Boden weg
Unwürdgem Raubbedürfnis nach,*
Und ruht tieftrauernd
Auf dem niedern Fels am Bach;
Er blickt zur Eich hinauf,
Hinauf zum Himmel,
Und eine Träne füllt sein hohes Aug.

Da kommt mutwillig durch die Myrtenäste
Dahergerauscht ein Taubenpaar,
Läßt sich herab und wandelt nickend
Über goldnen Sand am Bach,
Und rukt* einander an;
Ihr rötlich Auge buhlt umher,
Erblickt den Innigtrauernden.
Der Tauber* schwingt neugiergesellig sich
Zum nahen Busch und blickt
Mit Selbstgefälligkeit ihn freundlich an.
Du trauerst, liebelt er;
Sei gutes Mutes, Freund!

Hast du zur ruhigen Glückseligkeit
Nicht alles hier?
Kannst du dich nicht des goldnen Zweiges freun,
Der vor des Tages Glut dich schützt?
Kannst du der Abendsonne Schein
Auf weichem Moos am Bache nicht
Die Brust entgegenheben?
Du wandelst durch der Blumen frischen Tau,
Pflückst aus dem Überfluß
Des Waldgebüsches dir
Gelegne Speise, letzest
Den leichten Durst am Silberquell —
O Freund, das wahre Glück
Ist die Genügsamkeit,
Und die Genügsamkeit
Hat überall genug.
O Weise! sprach der Adler, und tief ernst
Versinkt er tiefer in sich selbst,
O Weisheit! Du redst wie eine Taube!*

Sennkraft: 'Sehnenkraft' ('Sehne': 'sinew'). *Raubbedürfnis nach*: the eagle can scarcely
fly even for the 'unworthy' purpose of catching its prey, as it needs to do to live (this
is in contrast with flying as an expression of sheer glory). *rukt*: 'coos'. *Der Tauber*:
'the male dove'. *wie eine Taube*: perhaps a reference to Matt. x. 16.

Written in 1774 or a little earlier. A fable, of a kind made popular in Ger-
many by the 'Aufklärer' Gellert, but directed against the comfortable
attitude often preached by such rationalists. The eagle represents the noble
aspirations of the 'Stürmer und Dränger'. The doves are particularly well
characterized: they swish boldly through the trees as though this were a
brave thing to do (one sees the pouting breast here); their 'reddish' eyes
(suggestive of degeneracy in a man) are on the look-out for someone to
lavish affection on ('buhlt'); and the male is made to look chummy with
'neugiergesellig', while his swift action ('schwingt sich') makes him look
a do-gooder. The image which the dove draws of the eagle devotedly raising
its bosom to the setting sun, while sitting on the moss by the stream, aptly
reveals his idea of glory. Lines 33–4, 47–8, 49–50, all spoken by the dove,
are pairs which form the equivalents of alexandrines, the French metre
which Goethe in his youth despised.

AN SCHWAGER KRONOS

IN DER POSTCHAISE DEN 10. OKTOBER 1774

Spude dich, Kronos!
Fort den rasselnden Trott!
Bergab gleitet der Weg;
Ekles Schwindeln zögert
Mir vor die Stirne dein Haudern.
Frisch den holpernden
Stock Wurzeln Steine den Trott
Rasch in's Leben hinein!

Nun schon wieder
Den eratmenden Schritt
Mühsam Berg hinauf.
Auf denn, nicht träge denn!
Strebend und hoffend an.

Weit hoch herrlich der Blick
Rings ins Leben hinein
Vom Gebürg zum Gebürg,
Über der ewige Geist
Ewigen Lebens ahndevoll.

Seitwärts des Überdachs Schatten
Zieht dich an
Und der Frischung verheißende Blick
Auf der Schwelle des Mädchens da. —
Labe dich! — Mir auch, Mädchen,
Diesen schäumenden Trunk
Und den freundlichen Gesundheitsblick!

Ab dann, frischer hinab!
Sieh, die Sonne sinkt.
Eh' sie sinkt, eh' mich faßt
Greisen im Moore Nebelduft,
Entzahnte Kiefer schnattern
Und das schlockernde Gebein —

Trunknen vom letzten Strahl
Reiß mich, ein Feuermeer
Mir im schäumenden Aug',
Mich Geblendeten, Taumelnden
In der Hölle nächtliches Tor!

Töne, Schwager, dein Horn,
Raßle den schallenden Trab,
Daß der Orkus vernehme, ein Fürst kommt,
Drunten von ihren Sitzen
Sich die Gewaltigen lüften.

In 1774 Goethe was on top of the world, beginning to realize, after the success of *Götz* and *Werther*, how much he might accomplish. Returning from a meeting with Klopstock, the reigning monarch in German poetry, he wrote in a post-chaise these verses, an allegory of life like the 'Mahomets-Gesang', but less grandiose, in fact off-hand, humorous, carefree.

Father Time (Kronos, or rather Chronos) is addressed as the coachman ('Schwager') and told to 'get cracking'. 'Spuden', a dialect word which Goethe spells with the Frankfurter's typical, soft 'd' for a 't' (just as he usually wrote 'Mädgen' for 'Mädchen'), means 'to hurry'. The coach comes downhill as Mahomet's river does, initially, but this time there is no easy course after birth. The language begins to break up under the strain of conveying Goethe's meaning not only grammatically but also 'bodily'. Lines 4–5 can be rearranged as 'dein Haudern zieht mir ekles Schwindeln vor die Stirne', but even this is a chaotically original way of saying that the slowness of the coach makes him dizzy. ('Haudern', later changed to the more familiar 'Zaudern', is another dialect word, meaning to travel in a hired vehicle, and hence to drive slowly—it is a personal insult to the coachman.) The end of the first section breaks up altogether as the nouns tumble out between 'holpernden' and the 'Trott' to which it belongs—the words are being slapped down on the page as they come to mind, without waiting to be shaped in the more grammatical form which Goethe was to give them in his final version. ('Frisch, holpert es gleich [i.e. ob-gleich (auch wenn) es holpert], über Stock und Steine den Trott rasch ins Leben hinein!'—which is still not impeccable.)

The upward course, surmounting life's difficulties, is toilsome in rhythm too, till the summit is reached with the superb gesture of 'Weit hoch herrlich der Blick'. Grammar is still disregarded—it is more important to get down the word 'über'—the spirit is *over*—than to formalize as Goethe did later by writing '*schwebet* der ewige Geist'. Similarly, as the thought of old age occurs, Goethe writes down 'eh' mich faßt Greisen'—letting the thought

make its impact just as it strikes him, whereas later he wrote 'Eh mich Greisen ergreift im Moore Nebelduft'. He is still using dialect with 'schlockernd' for 'schlotternd'—'my slummocking bones', as it were. And as he goes into the next section the first thought to strike him is that he is like a man drunk. 'Trunknen' goes down at once, to be rescued grammatically as well as may be by 'mich' in the next line: 'Reiß mich...mich Geblendeten, Taumelnden, etc...'.

The journey ends with a sweepingly comic exaggeration (half meant too, no doubt) as the princes of Hades (Orkus) are imagined rising from their seats to greet the new hero with some servility. By making this more polite, in his later version, Goethe altered the tone considerably:

> Daß der Orkus vernehme: wir kommen,
> Daß gleich an der Türe
> Der Wirt uns freundlich empfange.

The high spirits of the earlier sections needed an outrageous flourish to round them off. The new cosiness is not only feeble, it tends to suggest an unfortunately serious intention in the poem, a real welcome to a damnation which is at the same time not properly envisaged.

KENNER UND KÜNSTLER

KENNER

Gut, brav, mein Herr! Allein
Die linke Seite
Nicht ganz gleich der rechten!
Hier zuckt's ein wenig,
Und die Lippe
Nicht ganz Natur,
Noch alles so tot.

KÜNSTLER

O ratet, helft mir,
Daß ich mich vollende!
Wo ist der Urquell der Natur,
Daraus ich schöpfend
Himmel fühl' und Leben
In die Fingerspitzen empor,
Daß ich mit Göttersinn

Und Menschenhand
Vermög' zu bilden,
Was bei meinem Weib
Ich animalisch kann und muß?

<div align="center">KENNER</div>

Da sehen Sie zu.

<div align="center">KÜNSTLER</div>

So.

Included in a collection of poems for Frau von Stein, 1777. Goethe speaks
here of Art almost as a sexual procreation.

HARZREISE IM WINTER

Dem Geier gleich,
Der auf schweren Morgenwolken
Mit sanftem Fittich ruhend
Nach Beute schaut,
Schwebe mein Lied.

Denn ein Gott hat
Jedem seine Bahn
Vorgezeichnet,
Die der Glückliche
Rasch zum freudigen
Ziele rennt:
Wem aber Unglück
Das Herz zusammenzog,
Er sträubt vergebens
Sich gegen die Schranken
Des ehernen Fadens,
Den die doch bittre Schere*
Nur einmal löst.

<div align="center">55</div>

In Dickichts-Schauer
Drängt sich das rauhe Wild,
Und mit den Sperlingen
Haben längst die Reichen*
In ihre Sümpfe sich gesenkt.

Leicht ists folgen dem Wagen,
Den Fortuna führt,
Wie der gemächliche Troß
Auf gebesserten Wegen
Hinter des Fürsten Einzug.

Aber abseits wer ists?
Ins Gebüsch verliert sich sein Pfad,
Hinter ihm schlagen
Die Sträuche zusammen,
Das Gras steht wieder auf,
Die Öde verschlingt ihn.

Ach, wer heilet die Schmerzen
Des, dem Balsam zu Gift ward?
Der sich Menschenhaß
Aus der Fülle der Liebe trank?
Erst verachtet, nun ein Verächter,
Zehrt er heimlich auf
Seinen eignen Wert
In ungnügender Selbstsucht.

Ist auf deinem Psalter,
Vater der Liebe, ein Ton
Seinem Ohre vernehmlich,
So erquicke sein Herz!
Öffne den umwölkten Blick
Über die tausend Quellen
Neben dem Durstenden
In der Wüste.

Der du der Freuden viel schaffst,
Jedem ein überfließend Maß,

Segne die Brüder der Jagd
Auf der Fährte des Wilds
Mit jugendlichem Übermut
Fröhlicher Mordsucht,
Späte Rächer des Unbills,*
Dem schon Jahre vergeblich
Wehrt mit Knütteln der Bauer.

Aber den Einsamen hüll
In deine Goldwolken!
Umgib mit Wintergrün,
Bis die Rose wieder heranreift,
Die feuchten Haare,
O Liebe, deines Dichters!

Mit der dämmernden Fackel
Leuchtest du ihm
Durch die Furten bei Nacht,
Über grundlose Wege
Auf öden Gefilden;
Mit dem tausendfarbigen Morgen
Lachst du ins Herz ihm;
Mit dem beizenden Sturm
Trägst du ihn hoch empor;
Winterströme stürzen vom Felsen
In seine Psalmen,
Und Altar des lieblichsten Danks
Wird ihm des gefürchteten Gipfels
Schneebehangner Scheitel,
Den mit Geisterreihen
Kränzten ahnende Völker.

Du stehst mit unerforschtem Busen
Geheimnisvoll offenbar
Über der erstaunten Welt
Und schaust aus Wolken
Auf ihre Reiche und Herrlichkeit,
Die du aus den Adern deiner Brüder
Neben dir wässerst.

Schere: the Fates cut with scissors the thread of human life. *Die Reichen*: perhaps a misprint for 'die Reiher' (herons). *Unbills*: the reference is to the injustice done to the peasants by the game—including wild boars—preserved for the pleasure of the huntsmen.

Goethe climbed the Brocken in the Harz Mountains on 10 December 1777, during a tour undertaken partly to inspect mining villages, partly to comfort a hypochondriac named Plessing who had been depressed by *Werther*, partly because, as he wrote in his diary, the 'roof had been torn off his head' and he needed to achieve 'Reinheit'. To Frau von Stein he wrote that the real reason for the whole tour was to climb the Brocken, though he added, 'Sie wissen wie simbolisch mein daseyn ist', suggesting that to reach the summit would be a physical counterpart to the 'pure' condition of soul he hoped for. The poem was written during the tour. Throughout, it is strangely metaphorical and real at the same time. In contrast with 'An Schwager Kronos', where so much is allegorical, the words here can be almost limitlessly suggestive. (Goethe's dry comments in later years are in 'Die Kampagne in Frankreich' and in his Reply to Dr Kannegiesser.)

Goethe makes no clear distinctions: at times he feels himself a 'Geier'— probably a buzzard, though the word also means 'vulture' and 'kite'— at others he is closer to the wretched Plessing ('abseits, wer ists'), whose melancholia he knew at first hand. He feels both with the soaring bird of prey and with the man whom he wants to help. At other times he is 'der Einsame' making his way to the summit, to the place where his 'um-wölkter Blick' (in a dual sense) will give place to radiance. He not only needs the 'Vater der Liebe' but takes over that role himself towards another man. He has no clearly defined 'persona' of his own, and the difficulty of his language reflects this troubled state.

The first words have a savage feeling, as the poet looks around for his prey: they give the sense of ferocity in the mouth. From here he gropes his way into his subject, the contrast between the enjoyers of life and those who shrink from it, the first being associated with the fierce bird and the second with those who, in verse 3, cower and hide from it. This idea is developed in the first six verses, which read like an inward debate in Goethe as he thinks of his own following of 'Fortune's chariot' (it was two years now since he had come to Weimar) and the isolation which might have been his lot.

The seventh verse calls on the Father of Love to open up the clouds obscuring the melancholy man's vision, showing him the streams (of love or happiness) surrounding him—streams which in reality must have been obscured from Goethe himself in his climbing of the Brocken. The reference to Plessing is already being lost, and by the eighth verse Goethe is certainly thinking of his own loneliness at this instant. The 'Brüder der Jagd' are the Duke of Weimar and his entourage, whom Goethe had abandoned for the

sake of this ascent; they were now hunting the wild boars at long last (*späte* Rächer'), which had damaged the peasants' crops. From now on, Goethe is thinking of his own isolation, in contrast to the Duke and his company. He, the 'Dichter' of verse 9, is calling for help in his own perilous situation, physical and spiritual, recalling as he does so the benefits he has already received. These are not all pleasurable: there is rejoicing in the 'tausendfarbiger Morgen', but he is also carried aloft by the 'beizender Sturm', and *wintry* streams pour into his songs of praise. The ideas begin to resemble those in 'An den Mond', where both the rage and the tenderness of the river were to inspire the poet: a similar fusion of opposites seems to be in the offing. And this becomes more apparent at the summit itself. This was a place he had feared; it now becomes a place for loving thanks, although Goethe conceals somewhat his full knowledge of it. The Brocken is a place traditionally dedicated to evil, where the witches forgathered on the 'Walpurgisnacht'—it is the mountain which Faust ascends with the devil in search of revelations. Goethe knew of this, and in his letter to Frau von Stein was quite explicit: 'ich war oben heut und habe auf dem Teufels Altar meinem Gott den liebsten Danck geopfert'. But this meaning is not really obvious from the words of the poem. 'Geister-reihen', rather than 'Hexenreihen', almost looks like a concealment.

The last verse looks down from the summit with a strange commingling of mountain and god and poet, and with a suggestion, in the words 'auf ihre Reiche und Herrlichkeit', of the figure of Christ standing high above the world with the devil at his side (Matt. iv. 8). Is the sense towards which the poem is moving something to the effect that god and man, good and evil, fury and tenderness, are ultimately joined in one: is this the revela-tion Goethe was looking for? Certainly he was writing a few years later to his friend Lavater in these terms: 'In mir reinigt's sich unendlich und doch gesteh ich gerne Gott und Satan, Höll und Himmel, die du so schön bezeichnest, in mir Einem' (7 May 1781). But while the idea of a fusion of good and evil became a commonplace in German literature of the twentieth century (in Thomas Mann's work, for instance), it is still undefined in this earlier struggle for the depths of knowledge.

ILMENAU

AM 3. SEPTEMBER 1783

Anmutig Tal! du immergrüner Hain!
Mein Herz begrüßt euch wieder auf das beste;
Entfaltet mir die schwerbehangnen Äste,
Nehmt freundlich mich in eure Schatten ein,

Erquickt von euren Höhn, am Tag der Lieb und Lust,
Mit frischer Luft und Balsam meine Brust!
Wie kehrt ich oft mit wechselndem Geschicke,
Erhabner Berg! an deinen Fuß zurücke.
O laß mich heut an deinen sachten Höhn
Ein jugendlich, ein neues Eden sehn!
Ich hab es wohl auch mit um euch verdienet:
Ich sorge still, indes ihr ruhig grünet.

Laßt mich vergessen, daß auch hier die Welt
So manch Geschöpf in Erdefesseln hält,
Der Landmann leichtem Sand den Samen anvertraut
Und seinen Kohl dem frechen Wilde baut,
Der Knappe karges Brot in Klüften sucht,
Der Köhler zittert, wenn der Jäger flucht.
Verjüngt euch mir, wie ihr es oft getan,
Als fing' ich heut ein neues Leben an.

Ihr seid mir hold, ihr gönnt mir diese Träume,
Sie schmeicheln mir und locken alte Reime.
Mir wieder selbst, von allen Menschen fern,
Wie bad ich mich in euren Düften gern!
Melodisch rauscht die hohe Tanne wieder,
Melodisch eilt der Wasserfall hernieder;
Die Wolke sinkt, der Nebel drückt ins Tal,
Und es ist Nacht und Dämmrung auf einmal.

Im finstern Wald, beim Liebesblick der Sterne,
Wo ist mein Pfad, den sorglos ich verlor?
Welch seltne Stimmen hör ich in der Ferne?
Sie schallen wechselnd an dem Fels empor.
Ich eile sacht, zu sehn, was es bedeutet,
Wie von des Hirsches Ruf der Jäger still geleitet.

Wo bin ich? ists ein Zaubermärchen-Land?
Welch nächtliches Gelag am Fuß der Felsenwand?
Bei kleinen Hütten, dicht mit Reis bedecket,
Seh ich sie froh ans Feuer hingestrecket.

Es dringt der Glanz hoch durch den Fichten-Saal,
Am niedern Herde kocht ein rohes Mahl;
Sie scherzen laut, indessen, bald geleeret,
Die Flasche frisch im Kreise wiederkehret.

Sagt, wem vergleich ich diese muntre Schar?
Von wannen kommt sie? um wohin zu ziehen?
Wie ist an ihr doch alles wunderbar!
Soll ich sie grüßen? soll ich vor ihr fliehen?
Ist es der Jäger wildes Geisterheer?
Sinds Gnomen, die hier Zauberkünste treiben?
Ich seh im Busch der kleinen Feuer mehr;
Es schaudert mich, ich wage kaum, zu bleiben.
Ists der Ägyptier* verdächtiger Aufenthalt?
Ist es ein flüchtiger Fürst wie im Ardenner-Wald?*
Soll ich Verirrter hier in den verschlungnen Gründen
Die Geister Shakespeares gar verkörpert finden?
Ja, der Gedanke führt mich eben recht:
Sie sind es selbst, wo nicht ein gleich Geschlecht!
Unbändig schwelgt ein Geist in ihrer Mitten,
Und durch die Roheit fühl ich edle Sitten.

Wie nennt ihr ihn? Wer ists, der dort gebückt
Nachlässig stark die breiten Schultern drückt?
Er sitzt zunächst gelassen an der Flamme,
Die markige Gestalt aus altem Heldenstamme.
Er saugt begierig am geliebten Rohr,
Es steigt der Dampf an seiner Stirn empor.
Gutmütig trocken weiß er Freud und Lachen
Im ganzen Zirkel laut zu machen,
Wenn er mit ernstlichem Gesicht
Barbarisch bunt in fremder Mundart spricht.

Wer ist der andre, der sich nieder
An einen Sturz des alten Baumes lehnt
Und seine langen, feingestalten Glieder
Ekstatisch faul nach allen Seiten dehnt

Und, ohne daß die Zecher auf ihn hören,
Mit Geistesflug sich in die Höhe schwingt
Und von dem Tanz der himmelhohen Sphären
Ein monotones Lied mit großer Inbrunst singt?

Doch scheinet allen etwas zu gebrechen;
Ich höre sie auf einmal leise sprechen,
Des Jünglings Ruhe nicht zu unterbrechen,
Der dort am Ende, wo das Tal sich schließt,
In einer Hütte, leicht gezimmert,
Vor der ein letzter Blick des kleinen Feuers schimmert,
Vom Wasserfall umrauscht, des milden Schlafs genießt.
Mich treibt das Herz, nach jener Kluft zu wandern,
Ich schleiche still und scheide von den andern.

Sei mir gegrüßt, der hier in später Nacht
Gedankenvoll an dieser Schwelle wacht!
Was sitzest du entfernt von jenen Freuden?
Du scheinst mir auf was Wichtiges bedacht.
Was ists, daß du in Sinnen dich verlierest,
Und nicht einmal dein kleines Feuer schürest?

'O frage nicht! denn ich bin nicht bereit,
Des Fremden Neugier leicht zu stillen;
Sogar verbitt ich deinen guten Willen:
Hier ist zu schweigen und zu leiden Zeit.
Ich bin dir nicht imstande selbst zu sagen,
Woher ich sei, wer mich hierher gesandt;
Von fremden Zonen bin ich her verschlagen
Und durch die Freundschaft festgebannt.

Wer kennt sich selbst? wer weiß, was er vermag?
Hat nie der Mutige Verwegnes unternommen?
Und was du tust, sagt erst der andre Tag,
War es zum Schaden oder Frommen.
Ließ nicht Prometheus selbst die reine Himmelsglut
Auf frischen Ton vergötternd niederfließen?

Und konnt er mehr als irdisch Blut
Durch die belebten Adern gießen?
Ich brachte reines Feuer vom Altar;
Was ich entzündet, ist nicht reine Flamme.
Der Sturm vermehrt die Glut und die Gefahr,
Ich schwanke nicht, indem ich mich verdamme.

Und wenn ich unklug Mut und Freiheit sang
Und Redlichkeit und Freiheit sonder Zwang,
Stolz auf sich selbst und herzliches Behagen,
Erwarb ich mir der Menschen schöne Gunst;
Doch ach! ein Gott versagte mir die Kunst,
Die arme Kunst, mich künstlich zu betragen.
Nun sitz ich hier, zugleich erhoben und gedrückt,
Unschuldig und gestraft, und schuldig und beglückt.

Doch rede sacht! denn unter diesem Dach
Ruht all mein Wohl und all mein Ungemach:
Ein edles Herz, vom Wege der Natur
Durch enges Schicksal abgeleitet,
Das, ahnungsvoll, nun auf der rechten Spur
Bald mit sich selbst und bald mit Zauberschatten streitet
Und, was ihm das Geschick durch die Geburt geschenkt,
Mit Müh und Schweiß erst zu erringen denkt.
Kein liebevolles Wort kann seinen Geist enthüllen
Und kein Gesang die hohen Wogen stillen.

Wer kann der Raupe, die am Zweige kriecht,
Von ihrem künftgen Futter sprechen?
Und wer der Puppe, die am Boden liegt,
Die zarte Schale helfen durchzubrechen?
Es kommt die Zeit, sie drängt sich selber los
Und eilt auf Fittichen der Rose in den Schoß.

Gewiß, ihm geben auch die Jahre
Die rechte Richtung seiner Kraft.
Noch ist, bei tiefer Neigung für das Wahre,
Ihm Irrtum eine Leidenschaft.

Der Vorwitz lockt ihn in die Weite,
Kein Fels ist ihm zu schroff, kein Steg zu schmal;
Der Unfall lauert an der Seite
Und stürzt ihn in den Arm der Qual.
Dann treibt die schmerzlich überspannte Regung
Gewaltsam ihn bald da, bald dort hinaus,
Und von unmutiger Bewegung
Ruht er unmutig wieder aus.
Und düster wild an heitern Tagen,
Unbändig, ohne froh zu sein,
Schläft er, an Seel und Leib verwundet und zerschlagen,
Auf einem harten Lager ein:
Indessen ich hier, still und atmend kaum,
Die Augen zu den freien Sternen kehre
Und, halb erwacht und halb im schweren Traum,
Mich kaum des schweren Traums erwehre.'

Verschwinde, Traum!
 Wie dank ich, Musen, euch!
Daß ihr mich heut auf einen Pfad gestellet,
Wo auf ein einzig Wort die ganze Gegend gleich
Zum schönsten Tage sich erhellet;
Die Wolke flieht, der Nebel fällt,
Die Schatten sind hinweg. Ihr Götter, Preis und Wonne!
Es leuchtet mir die wahre Sonne,
Es lebt mir eine schönre Welt;
Das ängstliche Gesicht ist in die Luft zerronnen,
Ein neues Leben ists, es ist schon lang begonnen.

Ich sehe hier, wie man nach langer Reise
Im Vaterland sich wiederkennt,
Ein ruhig Volk in stillem Fleiße
Benutzen, was Natur an Gaben ihm gegönnt.
Der Faden eilet von dem Rocken*
Des Webers raschem Stuhle* zu,
Und Seil und Kübel wird in längrer Ruh
Nicht am verbrochnen Schachte* stocken;

Es wird der Trug entdeckt, die Ordnung kehrt zurück,
Es folgt Gedeihn und festes irdsches Glück.

So mög, o Fürst, der Winkel deines Landes
Ein Vorbild deiner Tage sein!
Du kennest lang die Pflichten deines Standes
Und schränkest nach und nach die freie Seele ein.
Der kann sich manchen Wunsch gewähren,
Der kalt sich selbst und seinem Willen lebt;
Allein wer andre wohl zu leiten strebt,
Muß fähig sein, viel zu entbehren.

So wandle du — der Lohn ist nicht gering —
Nicht schwankend hin, wie jener Sämann* ging,
Daß bald ein Korn, des Zufalls leichtes Spiel,
Hier auf den Weg, dort zwischen Dornen fiel;
Nein! streue klug wie reich, mit männlich steter Hand,
Den Segen aus auf ein geackert Land;
Dann laß es ruhn: die Ernte wird erscheinen
Und dich beglücken und die Deinen.

Ägyptier: 'gypsies'. *Ardenner-wald*: 'the forest of Arden'. *Rocken*: 'distaff'. *Stuhle*:
'loom' (usually 'Webstuhl'). *Schachte*: 'pitshaft'. *Sämann*: see Matt. xiii. 3.

Essentially a private poem, written for the twenty-sixth birthday of the
Duke Carl August, and including many personal references which the
Duke and his friends would have understood, though they are obscure to
modern readers, this is also, like the 'Harzreise', an account of a spiritual
progress. Goethe explained much of it to Eckermann on 23 October
1828 (see the *Conversations*).

The valley of the Ilm, beautifully evoked with its firs and gentle hills,
makes Goethe wish to forget the miseries of the Duke's subjects who live
there, and his wish is granted as he enters in v. 5 a dream-world which reminds
him of a gypsy encampment or that of the banished Duke in *As You Like It*.
He recognizes with amusement his friend Knebel, smoking a pipe, von
Seckendorff, humming, and then the Duke of Weimar himself ('der Jüng-
ling'). Watching over the Duke is Goethe's former self, who replies in some
distress to the present Goethe's questions. Goethe is calling to mind here
the wild life and sometimes heartless pranks he and the Duke had indulged
in a few years earlier, and his own 'Sturm und Drang' writings and

ambitions. He also speaks of his hopes that the Duke might emerge from his pupa-stage ('die Puppe') and develop his true nature. In all this part of the poem the youthful Goethe, affectionate, deeply troubled, humorous and almost boyish, is in evidence.

Rather forcibly, this musing is brought to an end with 'Verschwinde, Traum!' The situation had appeared rather desperate, and it had not been simply a dream—how then did the contentment of the present arise from the perplexities of the past? We are not told. The earlier life is not so much overcome as dismissed. The peasants and miners who were leading miserable lives at the beginning of the poem are suddenly said to be fully employed and contented. In the end, Goethe seems more concerned to make a tactful suggestion to the Duke about the running of his estates than to pursue his deeper problems any further. The hiatus here, the unsatisfying transition from the one state to the other, is all the more noticeable since the lines following the words 'Verschwinde, Traum!' are poetically flat. Up to this point, the metre has been mainly in iambic pentameters, Shakespearean metre, as Goethe and his contemporaries understood it. Occasionally, however, an alexandrine has crept in, at first rather rarely (like the tetrameters in 'Mahomets-Gesang'), then more frequently. The alexandrine was the French verse *par excellence*, anathema to the 'Sturm und Drang' and to Goethe too, for it almost always led to a rigid, monotonous beat when used in German. Now Goethe reverts to it, and as he comes closer to limiting 'die freie Seele', so he unconsciously uses the alexandrine more often. It occurs four times in the verse where the dream is bidden to vanish, and much more often in the last thirty lines than anywhere else, with the result that the would-be triumphant conclusion becomes lame, and as though not intended. The conventional phrase 'Ihr Götter, Preis und Wonne!' adds to this effect.

Thus Goethe's generosity, his willingness to consider the good of others as well as his own, does not serve him on this occasion in good stead. Despite several pleasing and amusing passages, 'Ilmenau' marks the beginning of a period when Goethe would only rarely write poetry of distinction. He has perhaps, like the poet Tasso in his play of that name, yielded too much in the end to his sense of social duty, although the wish for industrial reforms was praiseworthy. What should have marked a turning-point ends by being evasive and conventional, in contrast to the lively originality of the earlier part.

ZUEIGNUNG

Der Morgen kam; es scheuchten seine Tritte
Den leisen Schlaf, der mich gelind umfing,
Daß ich, erwacht, aus meiner stillen Hütte
Den Berg hinauf mit frischer Seele ging;
Ich freute mich bei einem jeden Schritte
Der neuen Blume, die voll Tropfen hing;
Der junge Tag erhob sich mit Entzücken,
Und alles war erquickt, mich zu erquicken.

Und wie ich stieg, zog von dem Fluß der Wiesen
Ein Nebel sich in Streifen sacht hervor;
Er wich und wechselte, mich zu umfließen,
Und wuchs geflügelt mir ums Haupt empor:
Des schönen Blicks sollt ich nicht mehr genießen,
Die Gegend deckte mir ein trüber Flor;
Bald sah ich mich von Wolken wie umgossen
Und mit mir selbst in Dämmrung eingeschlossen.

Auf einmal schien die Sonne durchzudringen,
Im Nebel ließ sich eine Klarheit sehn.
Hier sank er, leise sich hinabzuschwingen,
Hier teilt' er steigend sich um Wald und Höhn.
Wie hofft ich ihr den ersten Gruß zu bringen!
Sie hofft ich nach der Trübe doppelt schön.
Der luftge Kampf war lange nicht vollendet,
Ein Glanz umgab mich, und ich stand geblendet.

Bald machte mich, die Augen aufzuschlagen,
Ein innrer Trieb des Herzens wieder kühn,
Ich konnt es nur mit schnellen Blicken wagen,
Denn alles schien zu brennen und zu glühn.
Da schwebte, mit den Wolken hergetragen,
Ein göttlich Weib vor meinen Augen hin,
Kein schöner Bild sah ich in meinem Leben,
Sie sah mich an und blieb verweilend schweben.

Kennst du mich nicht? sprach sie mit einem Munde
Dem aller Lieb und Treue Ton entfloß:
Erkennst du mich, die ich in manche Wunde
Des Lebens dir den reinsten Balsam goß?
Du kennst mich wohl, an die, zu ewgem Bunde,
Dein strebend Herz sich fest und fester schloß.
Sah ich dich nicht mit heißen Herzenstränen
Als Knabe schon nach mir dich eifrig sehnen?

Ja! rief ich aus, indem ich selig nieder
Zur Erde sank, lang hab ich dich gefühlt;
Du gabst mir Ruh, wenn durch die jungen Glieder
Die Leidenschaft sich rastlos durchgewühlt;
Du hast mir wie mit himmlischem Gefieder
Am heißen Tag die Stirne sanft gekühlt;
Du schenktest mir der Erde beste Gaben,
Und jedes Glück will ich durch dich nur haben!

Dich nenn ich nicht. Zwar hör ich dich von vielen
Gar oft genannt, und jeder heißt dich *sein*,
Ein jedes Auge glaubt auf dich zu zielen,
Fast jedem Auge wird dein Strahl zur Pein.
Ach, da ich irrte, hatt ich viel Gespielen,
Da ich dich kenne, bin ich fast allein;
Ich muß mein Glück nur mit mir selbst genießen,
Dein holdes Licht verdecken und verschließen.

Sie lächelte, sie sprach: Du siehst, wie klug,
Wie nötig wars, euch wenig zu enthüllen!
Kaum bist du sicher vor dem gröbsten Trug,
Kaum bist du Herr vom ersten Kinderwillen,
So glaubst du dich schon Übermensch genug,
Versäumst die Pflicht des Mannes zu erfüllen!
Wieviel bist du von andern unterschieden?
Erkenne dich, leb mit der Welt in Frieden!

Verzeih mir, rief ich aus, ich meint es gut;
Soll ich umsonst die Augen offen haben?

Ein froher Wille lebt in meinem Blut,
Ich kenne ganz den Wert von deinen Gaben!
Für andre wächst in mir das edle Gut,
Ich kann und will das Pfund* nicht mehr vergraben!
Warum sucht ich den Weg so sehnsuchtsvoll,
Wenn ich ihn nicht den Brüdern zeigen soll?

Und wie ich sprach, sah mich das hohe Wesen
Mit einem Blick mitleidger Nachsicht an;
Ich konnte mich in ihrem Auge lesen,
Was ich verfehlt und was ich recht getan.
Sie lächelte, da war ich schon genesen,
Zu neuen Freuden stieg mein Geist heran;
Ich konnte nun mit innigem Vertrauen
Mich zu ihr nahn und ihre Nähe schauen.

Da reckte sie die Hand aus in die Streifen
Der leichten Wolken und des Dufts umher;
Wie sie ihn faßte, ließ er sich ergreifen,
Er ließ sich ziehn, es war kein Nebel mehr.
Mein Auge konnt im Tale wieder schweifen,
Gen Himmel blickt ich, er war hell und hehr.
Nur sah ich sie den reinsten Schleier halten,
Er floß um sie und schwoll in tausend Falten.

Ich kenne dich, ich kenne deine Schwächen,
Ich weiß, was Gutes in dir lebt und glimmt!
— So sagte sie, ich hör sie ewig sprechen, —
Empfange hier, was ich dir lang bestimmt;
Dem Glücklichen kann es an nichts gebrechen,
Der dies Geschenk mit stiller Seele nimmt:
Aus Morgenduft gewebt und Sonnenklarheit,
Der Dichtung Schleier aus der Hand der Wahrheit.

Und wenn es dir und deinen Freunden schwüle
Am Mittag wird, so wirf ihn in die Luft!
Sogleich umsäuselt Abendwindes Kühle,
Umhaucht euch Blumen-Würzgeruch und Duft.

Es schweigt das Wehen banger Erdgefühle,
Zum Wolkenbette wandelt sich die Gruft,
Besänftiget wird jede Lebenswelle,
Der Tag wird lieblich, und die Nacht wird helle.

So kommt denn, Freunde, wenn auf euren Wegen
Des Lebens Bürde schwer und schwerer drückt,
Wenn eure Bahn ein frischerneuter Segen
Mit Blumen ziert, mit goldnen Früchten schmückt,
Wir gehn vereint dem nächsten Tag entgegen!
So leben wir, so wandeln wir beglückt.
Und dann auch soll, wenn Enkel um uns trauern,
Zu ihrer Lust noch unsre Liebe dauern.

das Pfund: 'the talent' (cp. Matt. xxv. 14–30).

Written in August 1784 as an introduction to the epic poem *Die Geheim-nisse*, which Goethe never completed, this poem was later used by him as a dedicatory preface to his Collected Works, and has thus become very well known: the line 'Der Dichtung Schleier aus der Hand der Wahrheit' is proverbial now.

As in 'Harzreise im Winter' and 'Ilmenau', the theme is a revelation connected with the ascent of a hill or mountain. Where, however, the first of these was in free verse and the second in a mixture of blank verse and alexandrines, 'Zueignung' adopts a strictly classical form, that of Tasso's *Gerusalemme Liberata*: the 'ottava rima' or 'stanza', with its hendecasyllabics (here alternating with iambic pentameters), and its consistent rhyme-scheme *abababcc*. For the first time Goethe submits to a formal discipline.

The movement, however, is ponderous. The periphrasis in the first two lines sets the slow pace, although there is a sweetness, and a certain dignity too, in the gradual setting of the scene. The Italian form lends nobility, but also leads, for once, to a lack of concision. Pleonasms abound, and seem impossibly hard to justify: 'zu brennen und zu glühn'; 'der Erde beste Gaben, und jedes Glück'; 'verdecken und verschließen'; 'ich kann und will'; 'lebt und glimmt'; 'mich zu ihr nahn und ihre Nähe schauen'; 'der leichten Wolken und des Dufts'; 'Würzgeruch und Duft'. The imagery is almost entirely in cliché: balm is poured into wounds, the troubled brow is cooled, blessing comes in 'golden' fruits. The inadequacy of the poetry is most evident in the last verse of all, when the message has been revealed to the poet and one would want him to be writing at his best. Here a complete conventionality overtakes him. He speaks of 'life's burden', which is to be borne on 'ways' which also become a 'path', and

this path is both 'decorated' and 'ornamented' not only with flowers but with fruits. With this preparation the important line about going forward to meet the coming day, doing the task that lies to hand, is smothered—and not least by the line following, with its further pleonasm. Moreover, while the blessings of the expected new life sound good, they are vague, and the sudden introduction of the last couplet with 'Und dann auch' sounds forced. Both what Goethe says and the way he says it give the impression that he is making an empty gesture.

If this is so—and to maintain it of a poet of Goethe's greatness is at best audacious—it may have some connection with the nature of the message which it is the purpose of the poem to declare. The divine woman who appears in verse 4 is the symbol of an event deep in Goethe's experience. She is identical with the beautiful Natalie who appears, as though in a vision, to Wilhelm Meister, and with that 'sister' or 'wife' whom Goethe saw beyond and through Charlotte von Stein (see p. 22 above, 'Warum gabst du uns'). The dazzling radiance surrounding her recalls several moments in Faust's experience of a supernatural world. Here she appears with the simple and unambiguous name of Truth. But the poet's relation to her develops strangely. Having guessed her identity, he regrets that he must enjoy her presence alone, and is tempted to shut off her light from other men. The light of Truth is painful to behold ('wird dein Strahl zur Pein'), and thus, he feels, best concealed. For this, Truth chides him, bidding him realize how much like other men he is (the advice given to Tasso by Antonio at the end of Goethe's play), and at length he is persuaded. If his own eyes are open to Truth, he must allow other men to gain in vision too. At this point, however, Truth, while apparently approving his resolution, acts incongruously. She offers the poet a veil, made both of clarity and of 'Morgenduft'—that is, of those very mists which she draws aside with her hand to enable the poet to see the valley and the sky again. With this at his command, the poet will be able to bestow blessings on men. But while this may well accord with the idea that the whole Truth is not for mortal eyes to behold, it does contradict all that the poet looked for in the middle of the poem, namely that he should share his own open-eyed vision with other men. Truth seems to be behaving in a disturbingly deceptive way, and her notion of poetry as a magic veil whereby troubles can simply be made to vanish sounds at best sentimental. (In a letter of September 1786 Goethe used blunter language than this. Writing of the architect Palladio he found 'würcklich etwas göttliches in seinen Anlagen, völlig die Force des großen Dichters der aus Wahrheit und Lüge ein drittes bildet das uns bezaubert'. The extreme forms here, Truth and the Lie rather than Truth and morning mist, reflect the idea of polarity (see p. 49 above) and that of the divine as a fusion of opposites.)

The verdicts of a poet and of a scholar should not go unrecorded here. Goethe's elder, Wieland, wrote of this poem that he knew of 'nichts

Schöneres und nichts Vollkommneres in keiner Sprache' (letter of 12 November 1792), and Baumgart wrote: 'Der Eindruck der edlen Einfalt und stillen Größe klassischer Kunst geht von dem Gedicht aus und empfängt den Leser vom ersten Wort bis zum letzten.' Both these judgements would command a very great deal of assent.

Within the present section of poems, 'Zueignung' marks the point of resolution. Genius or demi-god? While Goethe speaks more calmly now, the answer is perhaps 'both': Prometheus *and* Ganymede, psalms of praise on the feared altar of the Brocken, songs of furious winter and of tender Spring, Truth *and* Delusion. One paradoxical effect on both his life and his poetry, unless Wieland was right, seems to have been for the time being an increase in conventionality.

HUMOROUS AND LIGHT VERSE

HUMOROUS AND LIGHT VERSE

There is an element of humour in much of Goethe's verse, especially in the early 1770's and in the late verse of the *West-östlicher Divan.* The poems in this section may help to emphasize this.

* * *

WUNSCH EINES JUNGEN MÄDCHENS

O fände für mich
Ein Bräutigam sich!
Wie schön ists nicht da,
Man nennt uns Mama.
Da braucht man zum Nähen,
Zur Schul nicht zu gehen;
Da kann man befehlen,
Hat Mägde, darf schmälen,
Man wählt sich die Kleider,
Nach Gusto* den Schneider;
Da läßt man spazieren,*
Auf Bälle sich führen,
Und fragt nicht erst lange
Papa und Mama.

Nach Gusto: according to taste. *Da läßt man spazieren*: understand 'man läßt sich spazieren führen'.

First published in 1768.

GUTE NACHT AN ANNETTEN,
DA SIE HEURATETE

Wenn man zwanzig Freier zählet,
Keinen liebt und alle quälet,

Alle liebt und keinen wählet,
Das ist eine stolze Lust
Für so eines Mädchens Brust.
Wenn so zwanzig bettlend stehn,
O wie lebt sichs da so schön!
Ist wohl eine Wollust größer?
Doch im Ehstand* sitzt man besser.

Zwar mit Freuden und mit Scherzen
In zwei kopulierten Herzen
Ists wie mit den Hochzeitkerzen.
Glänzend leuchten sie im Saal
Und verherrlichen das Mahl,
Aber so nach zehen Uhr
Bleiben kleine Stümpfchen nur;
Damit leuchte dir zu Bette!
Gute Nacht! Schlaf wohl, Annette!

Ehstand: 'the estate of marriage'.

Written about 1770.

STIRBT DER FUCHS, SO GILT DER BALG

Nach Mittage saßen wir
Junges Volk im Kühlen;
Amor kam, und *Stirbt der Fuchs*
Wollt er mit uns spielen.

Jeder meiner Freunde saß
Froh bei seinem Herzchen;
Amor blies die Fackel aus,
Sprach: Hier ist das Kerzchen!

Und die Fackel, wie sie glomm,
Ließ man eilig wandern,
Jeder drückte sie geschwind
In die Hand des andern.

76

Und mir reichte Dorilis
Sie mit Spott und Scherze;
Kaum berührt mein Finger sie,
Hell entflammt die Kerze,

Sengt mir Augen und Gesicht,
Setzt die Brust in Flammen,
Über meinem Haupte schlug
Fast die Glut zusammen.

Löschen wollt ich, patschte zu,
Doch es brennt beständig;
Statt zu sterben, ward der Fuchs
Recht bei mir lebendig.

Probably written in 1771 at Sesenheim. Goethe explains the game in a letter to Zelter of 4 May 1807: a smouldering taper (the fox) is passed from player to player, each of whom has to recite a verse beginning 'Stirbt der Fuchs …etc.') ('If the fox dies his skin is still useful'). The player left with the extinguished taper pays a forfeit. Goethe, however, far from being 'negligent' enough to let love die out, finds it bursting all too boldly into flame again.

REZENSENT*

Da hatt ich einen Kerl zu Gast,
Er war mir eben nicht zur Last;
Ich hatt just mein gewöhnlich Essen,
Hat sich* der Kerl pumpsatt* gefressen,
Zum Nachtisch, was ich gespeichert hatt.
Und kaum ist mir der Kerl so satt,
Tut ihn der Teufel zum Nachbar führen,
Über mein Essen zu räsonieren:*
'Die Supp hätt können gewürzter sein,
Der Braten brauner, firner* der Wein.'
Der Tausendsackerment!
Schlagt ihn tot, den Hund! Es ist ein Rezensent.

Rezensent: 'critic'. *Hat sich*: read 'da hat sich'. *pumpsatt*: either 'pumped full' or, just possibly, 'full at my expense' (cp. 'auf Pump', 'on tick'). *räsonieren*: 'to grumble'. *firn(-er)*: 'mature', especially of wine (contrast 'heurig').

Probably written about 1773. One of a large number of poems in which the young Goethe expressed dislike of critics (cp. 'Kenner und Künstler', p. 54). The rough 'Knittelverse' (rhyming lines of four stresses each), being associated with the poet Hans Sachs and other homely, honest folk, point the contrast with the critic's over-refinement.

KATECHISATION

LEHRER

Bedenk, o Kind! woher sind diese Gaben?
Du kannst nichts von dir selber haben.

KIND

Ei! Alles hab ich vom Papa.

LEHRER

Und der, woher hats der?

KIND

Vom Großpapa.

LEHRER

Nicht doch! Woher hats denn der Großpapa bekommen?

KIND

Der hats genommen.

Published 1773. Children were catechized in order to test their knowledge of religious dogma. Notice the alexandrine awarded to the teacher as a fitting metre for his pedantry.

Zwischen Lavater* und Basedow*
Saß ich bei Tisch des Lebens froh.
Herr Helfer,* der war gar nicht faul,
Setzt' sich auf einen schwarzen Gaul,

Nahm einen Pfarrer hinter sich
Und auf die Offenbarung strich,*
Die uns Johannes der Prophet
Mit Rätseln wohl versiegeln tät;
Er öffnet' die Siegel kurz und gut,
Wie man Theriaksbüchsen* öffnen tut,
Und maß mit einem heil'gen Rohr
Die Kubusstadt* und Perlentor*
Dem hocherstaunten Jünger vor.
 Ich war indes nicht weit gereist,
 Hatte ein Stück Salmen aufgespeist.
Vater Basedow, unter dieser Zeit,
Packt' einen Tanzmeister an seiner Seit'
Und zeigt' ihm, was die Taufe klar
Bei Christ und seinen Jüngern war,
Und daß sich's garnicht ziemet jetzt,
Daß man den Kindern die Köpfe netzt.
Drob* ärgert' sich der andre sehr
Und wollte garnichts hören mehr
Und sagt', es wüßte ein jedes Kind,
Daß's in der Bibel anders stünd'.
 Und ich behaglich unterdessen
 Hatt' einen Hahnen aufgefressen.

Und wie nach Emmaus* weiter ging's
Mit Sturm- und Feuerschritten:
Prophete rechts, Prophete links,
Das Weltkind in der Mitten.

Lavater (pronounced with a stress on each of the first two syllables): a Swiss 'Sturm und Drang' theologian (1741–1801) and close friend of Goethe's in his youth. *Basedow*: an educational theorist (1723–90) who believed, with Rousseau in 'natural' education and was opposed to infant baptism. *Herr Helfer*: Lavater was assistant priest at the Waisenhauskirche in Zürich. *auf die Offenbarung strich*: 'started up on (the Book of) Revelation' (of St John—'Johannes der Prophet'). *Theriaksbüchsen*: theriac, an antidote against snake-poison, was sold in boxes with an official seal. The Book of Revelation speaks of a book with seven seals, which is opened. *Kubusstadt, Perlentor*: these are referred to in Rev. xxi. 16 and 21. *Drob*: 'darob', 'darüber'. *Emmaus*: the place near which the risen Christ walked between two of his disciples (Luke xxiv. 13–35).

Written in 1774 during a journey along the Rhine, and also entitled 'Diner zu Koblenz' (see *Dichtung und Wahrheit*, book 14), this is a humorously tolerant account of the furious religious controversies of Goethe's friends, ending with a surprising parallel between himself as the 'Weltkind' (that is, the one who is quite content with earthly joys) and Christ as he appeared after the Resurrection. The suggestion is perhaps that the one who is really saved is the one who accepts gratefully what comes his way, without argument.

BEISPIEL

Wenn ich mal ungeduldig werde,
Denk ich an die Geduld der Erde,
Die, wie man sagt, sich täglich dreht
Und jährlich so wie jährlich geht.
Bin ich denn für was andres da? —
Ich folge der lieben Frau Mama.*

Frau Mama: cp. 'Mutter Erde'.

Published in 1815.

ERSCHAFFEN UND BELEBEN

Hans Adam war ein Erdenkloß,
Den Gott zum Menschen machte;
Doch bracht er aus der Mutter Schoß
Noch vieles Ungeschlachte.*

Die Elohim zur Nas hinein
Den besten Geist ihm bliesen;
Nun schien er schon was mehr zu sein,
Denn er fing an zu niesen.

Doch mit Gebein und Glied und Kopf
Blieb er ein halber Klumpen,
Bis endlich Noah für den Tropf
Das Wahre fand, den Humpen.

Der Klumpe fühlt sogleich den Schwung,
Sobald er sich benetzet,*

So wie der Teig durch Säuerung
Sich in Bewegung setzet.

So, Hafis,* mag dein holder Sang,
Dein heiliges Exempel
Uns führen, bei der Gläser Klang,
Zu unsres Schöpfers Tempel.

vieles Ungeschlachte: 'much that was uncouth'. *sich benetzet*: 'wets his whistle'.
Hafis: one of the most famous of Persian poets (1320–89).

Written on 21 June 1814 and published in the *West-östlicher Divan*, the collection of poems partly inspired by the Persian poet Hafiz. The ironical yet not unserious tone is typical of the *Divan*, though the effect of the singsong rhythm, suggesting, as it does in Hugo Wolf's accompaniment, a drunken head-wagging, is unique. The pedantic insistence on treating 'Elohim' (the Hebrew name of the divinity) as a plural is of a piece with this irony, and so is the reference to Noah as the discoverer of wine (*der Humpen* = the tankard; see Gen. ix. 21–5), and the reminder that Adam's mother's womb was made of earth. The 'heiliges Exempel' of Hafiz, a Muslim to whom alcohol was forbidden by his religion but who wrote many poems on the delights of wine, is in the same vein.

GENIALISCH TREIBEN

So wälz ich ohne Unterlaß,
Wie Sankt Diogenes, mein Faß.
Bald ist es Ernst, bald ist es Spaß;
Bald ist es Lieb, bald ist es Haß;
Bald ist es dies, bald ist es das;
Es ist ein Nichts und ist ein Was.
So wälz ich ohne Unterlaß,
Wie Sankt Diogenes, mein Faß.

Thought to have been written in Goethe's first years at Weimar, when he was still at times, as the title suggests, 'rollicking like a genius'. Diogenes the Greek philosopher lived in a barrel; he was not a saint and is not said to have rolled the barrel. Hugo Wolf's setting is rather intense, though no doubt Goethe also had some bitter experiences in mind when writing this poem. The continual rhyming on the same sound *can* be heard as a kind of desperate reiteration, yet Goethe is also evidently laughing at himself.

'Zu Goethes Denkmal was zahlst du jetzt?'
Fragt dieser, jener und der.—
Hätt ich mir nicht selbst ein Denkmal gesetzt,
Das Denkmal, wo käm es denn her?

* * *

Vom Vater hab ich die Statur,
Des Lebens ernstes Führen,
Vom Mütterchen die Frohnatur
Und Lust zu fabulieren.
Urahnherr war der Schönsten hold,
Das spukt* so hin und wieder;
Urahnfrau liebte Schmuck und Gold,
Das zuckt wohl durch die Glieder.
Sind nun die Elemente nicht
Aus dem Komplex zu trennen,
Was ist denn an dem ganzen Wicht
Original zu nennen?

spukt: literally 'haunts': 'I have a touch of that myself'.

Both from the 'Zahme Xenien', written 1823–8. The reference to the
elements recalls the passage in *Faust II*, ll. 11958–65.

Welch ein lustiges Spiel! Es windet am Faden die Scheibe,
 Die von der Hand entfloh, eilig sich wieder herauf!
Seht, so schein ich mein Herz bald dieser Schönen, bald jener
 Zuzuwerfen; doch gleich kehrt es im Fluge zurück.

One of the *Venezianische Epigramme* which were written in 1790 and 1794.
Perhaps the only poem in any language to develop the theme of the yo-yo.

'WELTANSCHAUUNGS-LYRIK'

'WELTANSCHAUUNGSLYRIK'

Between 1779 and 1783 Goethe wrote the four 'Hymnen' which follow. Like several of the poems written before he went to Weimar, they are in free verse in which a regular metre imperceptibly becomes more frequent as the poem proceeds. In 'Das Göttliche' there is no noticeable pattern for about fifteen lines, when a line running ⁄ × × ⁄ × begins to appear more and more often, till it dominates the middle of the poem. In 'Meine Göttin' there is no pattern for about twenty lines, when a line running × ⁄ × ⁄ × appears, to give way a little to ⁄ × × ⁄ × at the end. Both these rhythms characterize the other two 'Hymnen' also: in 'Gesang der Geister' there is × ⁄ × ⁄ × at first, but about half-way through ⁄ × × ⁄ × takes over; in 'Grenzen der Menschheit' ⁄ × × ⁄ × remains dominant throughout. ('I know', writes T. S. Eliot in 'The Music of Poetry' 'that a poem, or a passage of a poem, may tend to realize itself first as a particular rhythm before it reaches expression in words, and that this rhythm may bring to birth the idea and the image; and I do not believe that this is an experience peculiar to myself.')

It is untrue to say that these two rhythms are always associated in each case with a particular mood; however, × ⁄ × ⁄ × is a more lulling and gentle line in 'Gesang der Geister', while ⁄ × × ⁄ × tends to sound more bold and resolute in lines like 'Steht er mit festen | Markigen Knochen' or 'bald auch den kahlen | Schuldigen Scheitel'. It is interesting to see how the tendency towards a regular metre, which asserts itself fully in 'Zueignung' and in the *Römische Elegien*, develops in Goethe's early years at Weimar.

The effect of the three later 'Hymnen' has been compared to that of the choruses in Sophoclean tragedy, and they do seem well suited to choral speaking, the dactylic rhythms sometimes suggesting a drummed accompaniment. Interesting also is the comparison with the 'freie Rhythmen' of

Hölderlin, which, as Trunz says, are full of sudden surprises, with verse-endings which pause abruptly, sentences which end in the middle of a line: 'ein spröder Klang,' writes Trunz, 'der einer anderen, tragischeren seelischen Struktur entspricht'. There is often a swirl and swoop to Hölderlin's lines (as for instance in those beginning 'Versöhnender, der du nimmergeglaubt'), a breathlessness and intensity, very different from the stately, calm, more uniform pace of Goethe's free rhythms, even when he is speaking of disaster. In 'Grenzen der Menschheit' the voice rises twice on 'Uns hébt die Welle | Verschlíngt die Welle', and moves quietly down on 'Und wir versinken'. It does not shriek or groan. It announces with a solemnity of great open vowels that we live 'Nach ewigen, ehrnen | Großen Gesetzen', but it is not terrified, any more than it is when it recounts the fall of human lives 'Stufenweise | Zum Abgrund'. How final and unmoved this is, in comparison with the drawn-out, vertiginous cry at the end of Hölderlin's 'Hyperions Schiksaals Lied': 'Wie Wasser von Klippe | Zu Klippe geworfen | Jahrlang ins Ungewisse hinab'.

Goethe can be magisterial: 'Denn das allein | Unterscheidet ihn'; 'Denn unfühlend ist die Natur'; 'Denn mit Göttern | Soll sich nicht messen | Irgendein Mensch'; 'Denn uns allein | Hat er sie verbunden'. He can be almost conversational: 'Mit niemand streit ich'; he can joke about old Mother-in-Law Wisdom; he can be confidential: 'Doch kenn ich ihre Schwester', and provides an occasional touch of eighteenth-century sentiment unthinkable in Hölderlin: 'rosenbekränzt | Mit dem Lilienstengel'; 'das zarte Seelchen'; 'Und hat seine Freude | An der Törin'. On the whole, always excepting the first 'Hymne', 'Gesang der Geister', there is a marmoreal nobility, something akin to the sculptures of the age.

The meaning is not always consistent from poem to poem, and Goethe probably did not intend it to be. In 'Grenzen der Menschheit' the gods are set over against Man—he is within the river of life, of which they are spectators. In 'Das Göttliche', however, the gods are to be honoured as though, like men, they were helpful and good (and thus not indifferent

and remote). In the same poem Nature is called unfeeling, whereas in 'Gesang der Geister' the stars refresh themselves, lovingly it seems, in the calm surface of the river, and in 'Grenzen der Menschheit' even the lightning is regarded as a blessing to mankind. It is tempting to think, therefore, that the 'Hymnen' are once again (see p. 41) dramatic utterances rather than personal confessions. The difficulty here is that there are also discrepancies within individual poems. In 'Das Göttliche', while verse 5 attributes events to blind chance, verse 6 at once and without explanation speaks of our submission to eternal laws. In 'Meine Göttin' Phantasy is said to be both tender and savagely forbidding (the idea of polarity (see p. 49) may have influenced this), but by the end the second quality seems forgotten, and she remains only as the 'spoiled darling' and the 'delicate little soul'. It may be that Goethe had no wish to reconcile his statements of belief, that they were all aspects of himself which he would express as part of the Whole, itself a kind of great stage-play. But this cannot be reconciled with the great moral injunctions of 'Das Göttliche'.

* * *

GESANG DER GEISTER ÜBER DEN WASSERN

Des Menschen Seele
Gleicht dem Wasser:
Vom Himmel kommt es,
Zum Himmel steigt es,
Und wieder nieder
Zur Erde muß es,
Ewig wechselnd.

Strömt von der hohen,
Steilen Felswand
Der reine Strahl,
Dann stäubt er lieblich

In Wolkenwellen
Zum glatten Fels,
Und leicht empfangen
Wallt er verschleiernd,
Leisrauschend
Zur Tiefe nieder.

Ragen Klippen
Dem Sturz entgegen,
Schäumt er unmutig
Stufenweise
Zum Abgrund.

Im flachen Bette
Schleicht er das Wiesental hin,
Und in dem glatten See
Weiden ihr Antlitz
Alle Gestirne.

Wind ist der Welle
Lieblicher Buhler;
Wind mischt vom Grund aus
Schäumende Wogen.

Seele des Menschen,
Wie gleichst du dem Wasser!
Schicksal des Menschen,
Wie gleichst du dem Wind!

Written 9–11 October 1779 in Lauterbrunnen, where there is a well-known, extremely high waterfall. The original title was 'Gesang der lieblichen Geister in der Wüste', and the lines were a dialogue, divided between 'Erster Geist' and 'Zweiter Geist', thus giving the effect of a dramatic piece in which the spirits converse, rather than of a lyrical utterance by the poet himself. The rhythm has a sinuous beauty in the opening and closing verses, and varies with the movement of the water in verses 2 and 3.

Some take the opening to mean that man enters life in cycle after cycle, others that he has joyful and sad experiences within one life. The former perhaps fits the symbolism of the whole poem better. The last two verses are taken by Viktor Hehn to mean that Destiny plays with man as it pleases.

However, this is difficult to reconcile with the 'lieblicher Buhler', and Goethe may have intended that love unites all men in one, just as the wind mixes the waters at the bed of the river ('vom Grund aus') with those at the surface. (Although the wind does not seem to do this in reality.) The last two verses are difficult, possibly, because of their briefness and because they do not proceed organically from the earlier ones.

MEINE GÖTTIN

Welcher Unsterblichen
Soll der höchste Preis sein?
Mit niemand streit ich,
Aber ich geb ihn
Der ewig beweglichen,
Immer neuen,
Seltsamen Tochter Jovis,*
Seinem Schoßkinde,
Der Phantasie.

Denn ihr hat er
Alle Launen,
Die er sonst nur allein
Sich vorbehält,
Zugestanden
Und hat seine Freude
An der Törin.

Sie mag rosenbekränzt
Mit dem Lilienstengel
Blumentäler betreten,
Sommervögeln gebieten
Und leichtnährenden Tau
Mit Bienenlippen
Von Blüten saugen;

Oder sie mag
Mit fliegendem Haar
Und düsterm Blicke
Im Winde sausen

Um Felsenwände,
Und tausendfarbig,
Wie Morgen und Abend,
Immer wechselnd
Wie Mondesblicke,*
Den Sterblichen scheinen.

Laßt uns alle
Den Vater preisen!
Den alten, hohen,
Der solch eine schöne,
Unverwelkliche Gattin
Dem sterblichen Menschen
Gesellen mögen!

Denn uns allein
Hat er sie verbunden
Mit Himmelsband
Und ihr geboten,
In Freud und Elend
Als treue Gattin
Nicht zu entweichen.

Alle die andern
Armen Geschlechter
Der kinderreichen,
Lebendigen Erde
Wandeln und weiden
In dunkelm Genuß
Und trüben Schmerzen
Des augenblicklichen
Beschränkten Lebens,
Gebeugt vom Joche
Der Notdurft.

Uns aber hat er
Seine gewandteste,
Verzärtelte Tochter,
Freut euch! gegönnt.

Begegnet ihr lieblich,
Wie einer Geliebten!
Laßt ihr die Würde
Der Frauen* im Haus!

Und daß die alte
Schwiegermutter Weisheit
Das zarte Seelchen
Ja nicht beleidge!
Doch kenn ich ihre Schwester,
Die ältere, gesetztere,
Meine stille Freundin:
O daß die erst*
Mit dem Lichte des Lebens
Sich von mir wende,
Die edle Treiberin,
Trösterin Hoffnung!

Jovis: 'of Jove'. *Mondesblicke*: 'glimpses of the moon'. *Der Frauen* is here singular.
O daß die erst...: the sense is 'O may she not leave me till life leaves me'.

Sent with a letter to Frau von Stein on 15 September 1780, just after it had
been written. The tone is a little coy and prim. (See also the introduction to
this section.)

GRENZEN DER MENSCHHEIT*

Wenn der uralte,
Heilige Vater
Mit gelassener Hand
Aus rollenden Wolken
Segnende Blitze
Über die Erde sät,
Küss' ich den letzten
Saum seines Kleides,*
Kindliche Schauer
Treu in der Brust.

Denn mit Göttern
Soll sich nicht messen
Irgendein Mensch.
Hebt er sich aufwärts
Und berührt
Mit dem Scheitel die Sterne,
Nirgends haften dann
Die unsichern Sohlen,
Und mit ihm spielen
Wolken und Winde.

Steht er mit festen,
Markigen Knochen
Auf der wohlgegründeten
Dauernden Erde,
Reicht er nicht auf,
Nur mit der Eiche
Oder der Rebe
Sich zu vergleichen.

Was unterscheidet
Götter von Menschen?
Daß viele Wellen
Vor jenen wandeln,
Ein ewiger Strom:
Uns hebt die Welle,
Verschlingt die Welle,
Und wir versinken.

Ein kleiner Ring
Begrenzt unser Leben,
Und viele Geschlechter
Reihen sich dauernd
An ihres Daseins
Unendliche Kette.

Menschheit: the word here means 'Menschenwesen', 'Menschsein', not, as it does today, 'alle Menschen, die menschliche Gesellschaft der ganzen Erde', to quote Brockhaus. *Saum seines Kleides*: possibly a reference to Matt. ix. 20.

Written in 1781 at the latest. Although this is one of Goethe's best known poems, its manner conceals neglectful thought. The poet affirms that he worships humbly, even when God calmly scatters his lightnings: these are blessings, and perhaps in some sense seeds, since they are said to be sown, but the sense of this is not made apparent. Then a reason is given for this childlike loyalty: Man ought not to contend with the gods (by accusing them, perhaps, of injustice?), since if he tries to reach heaven he loses contact with earth, and if he remains on earth he cannot compare with the oak or the vine. The second part of this argument is weak, the oak and the vine having no obvious relevance (Man is superior in some ways to both). The first part is understandable in physical terms, but it is not apparent what the physical image is intended to symbolize, or what it has to do with the necessity for Man not to question the ways of the gods: the argument seems too closely bound to mere questions of physical size. Having made these affirmations, the poet breaks off, and starts in the last two verses a completely different theme, that the distinction between gods and men resides in the immortality of the one and the mortality of the other. This has no connection with the original issue, so far as this concerned the justification of the ways of the gods. Rhythmically, however, the poem is majestic.

DAS GÖTTLICHE

Edel sei der Mensch,
Hilfreich und gut!
Denn das allein
Unterscheidet ihn
Von allen Wesen,
Die wir kennen.

Heil den unbekannten
Höhern Wesen,
Die wir ahnen!
Ihnen gleiche der Mensch;
Sein Beispiel lehr uns
Jene glauben.

Denn unfühlend
Ist die Natur:
Es leuchtet die Sonne*
Über Bös' und Gute,

Und dem Verbrecher
Glänzen wie dem Besten
Der Mond und die Sterne.

Wind und Ströme,
Donner und Hagel
Rauschen ihren Weg
Und ergreifen
Vorüber eilend
Einen um den andern.

Auch so das Glück
Tappt unter die Menge,
Faßt bald des Knaben
Lockige Unschuld,
Bald auch den kahlen
Schuldigen Scheitel.

Nach ewigen, ehrnen,
Großen Gesetzen
Müssen wir alle
Unseres Daseins
Kreise vollenden.

Nur allein der Mensch
Vermag das Unmögliche:
Er unterscheidet,
Wählet und richtet;
Er kann dem Augenblick
Dauer verleihen.

Er allein darf
Den Guten lohnen,
Den Bösen strafen,
Heilen und retten,
Alles Irrende, Schweifende
Nützlich verbinden.

Und wir verehren
Die Unsterblichen,
Als wären sie Menschen,
Täten im Großen,
Was der Beste im Kleinen
Tut oder möchte.

Der edle Mensch
Sei hilfreich und gut!
Unermüdet schaff er
Das Nützliche, Rechte,
Sei uns ein Vorbild
Jener geahneten Wesen!

Es leuchtet die Sonne... : cp. Matt. v. 45.

Probably written 1783. Published 1785 in Jacobi's *Über die Lehren des Spinosa*. Although the poem is well intentioned, it is not always clear. It seems uncertain what part is left for the gods, since Man is said to judge, reward and punish, and the realm of Nature is evidently not under the divine control (not, at least, in this poem: compare, however, the beginning of 'Grenzen der Menschheit'). See also the introduction to this section (p. 87).

EARLY FOLK-SONGS
AND BALLADS

EARLY FOLK-SONGS AND BALLADS

Bishop Percy published his *Reliques of Ancient English Poetry*, largely consisting of folk-songs and ballads, in 1765. They had a strong appeal in Germany, where the idea of a literature with national roots was gaining support: folk-songs were an admirable place in which to look for such roots. Herder, who invented the word 'Volkslied', published his essay 'Ossian und die Lieder alter Völker' in 1773 (including, incidentally, Goethe's 'Heidenröslein' as Herder remembered it, but calling it 'ein älteres deutsches Lied'). Goethe collected folk-songs in Alsace in 1771. Herder's own collection, *Stimmen der Völker*, including songs from many parts of the world, was published in 1778-9. The Romantic poets Brentano and Arnim published theirs, in 1805-8, as *Des Knaben Wunderhorn*.

The word 'folk-song' is often used synonymously with 'ballad', although there are many folk-songs with no narrative element. Other ballad-writers of Goethe's times include Bürger, Schiller, Uhland, Chamisso and Heine. Their ballads are, however, as a rule historical in their setting and more polished than many of the songs which the people themselves were singing or hearing. Bürger's 'Lenore' probably comes closest to the 'Moritaten', once sung by a man pointing to a large scroll, on which pictures of the sensational events in his story had been painted. These were in those days the poor man's newspaper, with titles like 'Blutschande und vierfacher Kindermord', 'Die Husarenbraut oder: Treue Liebe bis zum Tode' and 'Gedanken über die den 20. Juni 1776 an einem 14jährigen Bauernmädchen ohnweit München, neben der Landsberger Straße, ausgeübte erschreckliche Mordtat, durch ein Lied entworfen'. (All of these are in *Lob der Träne*, ed. K. H. Kramer, Berlin, 1955.) Some further idea of the folk-song, as distinct from the 'Moritat', can be gained from the collection *Der Zupfgeigenhansl*, ed. Hans Breuer (1908), and often reprinted (with music).

It was a matter of some consequence whether the cultured poet could re-create poetry for the people, in genuine contact with them (as Werther sought to be in his meeting with the village-girl at the well). But even today 'poetry in pubs' is something of a freak. Several of Goethe's folk-songs are known throughout Germany and all over the world, and yet even these sometimes have the stamp of literature still—it is a very rare thing for a great poet to have the common touch completely.

* * *

HEIDENRÖSLEIN

Sah ein Knab ein Röslein stehn,
Röslein auf der Heiden,
War so jung und morgenschön,
Lief er schnell, es nah zu sehn,
Sahs mit vielen Freuden.
Röslein, Röslein, Röslein rot,
Röslein auf der Heiden.

Knabe sprach: Ich breche dich,
Röslein auf der Heiden!
Röslein sprach: Ich steche dich,
Daß du ewig denkst an mich,
Und ich wills nicht leiden.
Röslein, Röslein, Röslein rot,
Röslein auf der Heiden.

Und der wilde Knabe brach
's Röslein auf der Heiden;
Röslein wehrte sich und stach,
Half ihm doch kein Weh und Ach,
Mußt es eben leiden.
Röslein, Röslein, Röslein rot,
Röslein auf der Heiden.

Written in 1771. There is an old folk-song in which the line 'Röslein auf der Heiden' is repeated, but without further similarity to Goethe's poem.

In the latter there is sometimes thought to be a hint of Goethe's feeling of guilt at having abandoned Friederike Brion, but if there is any allegory it points rather to importunacy: the boy does not *abandon* the rose. The language, with its omissions of the definite article and of the personal pronoun, is not truly typical of the folk-song but rather of the eighteenth-century gentleman's pleasure in artlessness. Goethe's poem, however, especially in Schubert's setting, is better known today than any of the folk-songs.

DAS VEILCHEN

Ein Veilchen auf der Wiese stand,
Gebückt in sich und unbekannt;
Es war ein herzig's Veilchen.
Da kam eine junge Schäferin
Mit leichtem Schritt und munterm Sinn
Daher, daher,
Die Wiese her, und sang.

Ach! denkt das Veilchen, wär' ich nur
Die schönste Blume der Natur,
Ach, nur ein kleines Weilchen,
Bis mich das Liebchen abgepflückt
Und an dem Busen matt gedrückt!
Ach nur, ach nur
Ein Viertelstündchen lang!

Ach, aber ach! Das Mädchen kam
Und nicht in acht das Veilchen nahm,
Ertrat's, das arme Veilchen.
Und sank und starb und freut sich noch:
Und sterb' ich denn, so sterb ich doch
Durch sie, durch sie,
Zu ihren Füßen doch!

Written 1773–4 as a song in the 'Singspiel' *Erwin und Elmire*, a dainty Rococo entertainment in the spirit of Mozart (who did in fact set the song to music). It is not a ballad at all in the sense of the folk-song ballad,

though it has a pretty, musical quality, especially in the refrain. A recent commentator suggests that it expresses Goethe's pantheism, but that is nonsense; it is simply a light-hearted trifle.

DER KÖNIG IN THULE

Es war ein König in Thule*
Gar treu bis an das Grab,
Dem sterbend seine Buhle*
Einen goldnen Becher gab.

Es ging ihm nichts darüber,
Er leert' ihn jeden Schmaus;
Die Augen gingen ihm über,*
So oft er trank daraus.

Und als er kam zu sterben,
Zählt' er seine Städt' im Reich,
Gönnt' alles seinen Erben,
Den Becher nicht zugleich.

Er saß beim Königsmahle,
Die Ritter um ihn her,
Auf hohem Vätersaale,
Dort auf dem Schloß am Meer.

Dort stand der alte Zecher,
Trank letzte Lebensglut,
Und warf den heilgen Becher
Hinunter in die Flut.

Er sah ihn stürzen, trinken
Und sinken tief ins Meer.
Die Augen täten ihm sinken;
Trank nie einen Tropfen mehr.

Thule: 'ultima Thule' was for the Romans the farthest point to the North. *Buhle*: 'mistress'. *gingen ihm über*: 'overflowed'.

Written in 1774, more truly in the spirit of the older folk-songs. Goethe gave it to Gretchen to sing in *Faust*, its theme of undying love being well suited to her, although there is dramatic irony in it too, since she cannot guess how Faust is to betray and abandon her. Gretchen might not appreciate, either, the touch of humour in the reference to the King as 'the old toper'.

The present version is smoother than the original one, in which Goethe reproduced a rougher speech of the people, as he did in *Götz* occasionally. (Verse 1 read: 'Es war ein König in Thule | Ein' goldnen Becher er hätt | Empfangen von seiner Buhle | Auf ihrem Todesbett'.) The present verse 6 improves on Goethe's earlier versions in its rhythmic presentation of the lilting movement of the goblet in the sea, before it fills up and plunges to the bottom. The whole poem is wonderfully compact and evocative, musically alive. Of several settings, Schubert's is the best known.

GRETCHEN AM SPINNRAD

Meine Ruh' ist hin,
Mein Herz ist schwer;
Ich finde sie nimmer
Und nimmermehr.

Wo ich ihn nicht hab',
Ist mir das Grab,
Die ganze Welt
Ist mir vergällt.

Mein armer Kopf
Ist mir verrückt,
Mein armer Sinn
Ist mir zerstückt.

Meine Ruh' ist hin,
Mein Herz ist schwer;
Ich finde sie nimmer
Und nimmermehr.

Nach ihm nur schau' ich
Zum Fenster hinaus,
Nach ihm nur geh' ich
Aus dem Haus.

Sein hoher Gang,
Sein' edle Gestalt,
Seines Mundes Lächeln,
Seiner Augen Gewalt,

Und seiner Rede
Zauberfluß,
Sein Händedruck,
Und ach sein Kuß!

Meine Ruh' ist hin,
Mein Herz ist schwer;
Ich finde sie nimmer
Und nimmermehr.

Mein Busen drängt
Sich nach ihm hin.
Ach dürft' ich fassen
Und halten ihn,

Und küssen ihn
So wie ich wollt',
An seinen Küssen
Vergehen sollt'!

Also sung by Gretchen in *Faust*, when her lover has momentarily abandoned her, although it can stand completely alone as a poem of utter simplicity of language and feeling, such as a girl of the people might sing. The exceptional quality is the urgent rhythm, with the recurring, insistent refrain: in the first recorded version, in the *Urfaust*, this led to a final outburst of irresistible yearning, beginning 'Mein Schoß, Gott! drängt | Sich nach ihm hin', and running the last two verses together into one, in a flood of passion. The present, later version, though identical in all other ways except for a few commas, ends more serenely. As Goethe first conceived it, the poem was a dramatic realization of a girl's bewildered, bodily surrender, and very little of this is changed.

DER FISCHER

Das Wasser rauscht', das Wasser schwoll,
Ein Fischer saß daran,
Sah nach dem Angel ruhevoll,
Kühl bis ans Herz hinan.
Und wie er sitzt und wie er lauscht,
Teilt sich die Flut empor;
Aus dem bewegten Wasser rauscht
Ein feuchtes Weib hervor.

Sie sang zu ihm, sie sprach zu ihm:
Was lockst du meine Brut
Mit Menschenwitz und Menschenlist
Hinauf in Todesglut?
Ach wüßtest du, wie's Fischlein ist
So wohlig auf dem Grund,
Du stiegst herunter, wie du bist,
Und würdest erst gesund.

Labt sich die liebe Sonne nicht,
Der Mond sich nicht im Meer?
Kehrt wellenatmend ihr Gesicht
Nicht doppelt schöner her?
Lockt dich der tiefe Himmel nicht,
Das feuchtverklärte* Blau?
Lockt dich dein eigen Angesicht
Nicht her in ewgen Tau?

Das Wasser rauscht', das Wasser schwoll,
Netzt' ihm den nackten Fuß;
Sein Herz wuchs ihm so sehnsuchtsvoll,
Wie bei der Liebsten Gruß.
Sie sprach zu ihm, sie sang zu ihm;
Da wars um ihn geschehn:
Halb zog sie ihn, halb sank er hin,
Und ward nicht mehr gesehn.

feuchtverklärt: 'transfigured by the water'—but the German has overtones of 'Klarheit' which no English phrase can render.

Written in 1778. Speaking to Eckermann on 3 November 1823, Goethe deprecated attempts at painting the incident in this poem: 'Es ist ja in dieser Ballade bloß das Gefühl des Wassers ausgedrückt, das Anmutige, das uns im Sommer lockt, uns zu baden.' There is more to it than this, for one does not bathe in order to drown oneself, but perhaps Romantic readers had been too prone to see here an allegory of the fatal attraction of the depths, which is certainly hinted at in the poem, though in a different mood from that of Fouqué's *Undine*, or Andersen's *Mermaid*, or Keats' 'La Belle Dame sans Merci'. There are hypnotic passages (especially in the repetitive parts) and sensual ones, but no terror, no thrill of abandonment, no drear place of appointment where 'no birds sing', rather a repleteness and satisfaction in the fisher, who is unresisting, while the mermaid is quite homely at times, with ''s Fischlein' and 'wohlig'. (Goethe shocked Frau von Stein by telling her that 'Todesglut' meant the frying-pan, not the sunshine.) The mermaid could be speaking with Goethe's own voice in verse 3, especially with 'wellenatmend' and 'feuchtverklärt'. Yet this cannot be quite the case, for though she appeals to the universe to confirm her temptation, the love to which the fisher finally succumbs is that of a Narcissus: he falls in love with his own reflection. The poem is plainer in its rhythm than a folk-ballad, but more complex in meaning.

ERLKÖNIG*

Wer reitet so spät durch Nacht und Wind?
Es ist der Vater mit seinem Kind;
Er hat den Knaben wohl in dem Arm,
Er faßt ihn sicher, er hält ihn warm.

Mein Sohn, was birgst du so bang dein Gesicht? —
Siehst, Vater, du den Erlkönig nicht?
Den Erlenkönig mit Kron und Schweif? —
Mein Sohn, es ist ein Nebelstreif. —

'Du liebes Kind, komm, geh mit mir!
Gar schöne Spiele spiel ich mit dir;
Manch bunte Blumen sind an dem Strand,
Meine Mutter hat manch gülden Gewand.'

Mein Vater, mein Vater, und hörest du nicht,
Was Erlkönig mir leise verspricht? —

Sei ruhig, bleibe ruhig, mein Kind;
In dürren Blättern säuselt der Wind. —

'Willst, feiner Knabe, du mit mir gehn?
Meine Töchter sollen dich warten* schön;
Meine Töchter führen den nächtlichen Reihn,
Und wiegen und tanzen und singen dich ein.'

Mein Vater, mein Vater, und siehst du nicht dort
Erlkönigs Töchter am düstern Ort? —
Mein Sohn, mein Sohn, ich seh es genau:
Es scheinen die alten Weiden so grau. —

'Ich liebe dich, mich reizt deine schöne Gestalt;
Und bist du nicht willig, so brauch ich Gewalt.'
Mein Vater, mein Vater, jetzt faßt er mich an!
Erlkönig hat mir ein Leids getan! —

Dem Vater grausets, er reitet geschwind,
Er hält in Armen das ächzende Kind,
Erreicht den Hof mit Müh und Not;
In seinen Armen das Kind war tot.

Erlkönig: 'King of the Alders'. *dich warten*: understand 'auf dich warten'.

Written in 1782, the most dramatic and intense of all Goethe's ballads, marvellously characterized. The terror of the child comes through most of all in his 'mein Vater, mein Vater', repeated hastily in almost every speech. The King speaks first with a whispering allurement which turns into a screech of possessive love, while the gruff confidence of the father is expressed very much in the long slow words 'Mein Sohn, mein Sohn', 'Sei ruhig, bleibe ruhig', which hold up the pace from time to time until in the last verse but one the child's shriek releases the full gallop.

Originally included in Goethe's 'Singspiel', *Die Fischerin*, the poem was suggested by Herder's translation of a Danish ballad, 'Ellerkongen' ('The Elf-King'). Whether deliberately or not, Goethe made his version ('The Alder-King') suggest the fearful shapes seen by travellers in the mists—alders commonly grow in marshy places and by rivers, where mists are frequent. The theme of the fatal attraction of the elements is akin to that of 'Der Fischer'.

This is another of Schubert's best known songs.

DER UNTREUE KNABE

Es war ein Buhle frech genung,
War erst aus Frankreich kommen,
Der hat ein armes Maidel jung
Gar oft in Arm genommen,
Und liebgekost und liebgeherzt,
Als Bräutigam herumgescherzt,
Und endlich sie verlassen.

Das arme Maidel das erfuhr,
Vergingen ihr die Sinnen,
Sie lacht' und weint' und bet' und schwur —
So fuhr die Seel' von hinnen.
Die Stund, da sie verschieden war,
Wird bang dem Buben, graust sein Haar,
Es treibt ihn fort zu Pferde.

Er gab die Sporen kreuz und quer
Und ritt auf alle Seiten,
Herüber, 'nüber, hin und her,
Kann keine Ruh' erreiten;*
Reit' sieben Tag und sieben Nacht —
Es blitzt und donnert, stürmt und kracht,
Die Fluten reißen über;

Und reit' im Blitz und Wetterschein
Gemäuerwerk entgegen,
Bindt's Pferd hauß an* und kriecht hinein
Und duckt sich vor dem Regen.
Und wie er tappt und wie er fühlt,
Sich unter ihm die Erd' erwühlt:
Er stürzt wohl hundert Klafter.*

Und als er sich ermannt vom Schlag,
Sieht er drei Lichtlein schleichen.
Er rafft sich auf und krapelt* nach,

Die Lichtlein ferne weichen,
Irrführen ihn die Quer und Läng',
Treppauf treppab durch enge Gäng',
Verfallne wüste Keller.

Auf einmal steht er hoch im Saal,
Sieht sitzen hundert Gäste,
Hohlaugig grinsen allzumal
Und winken ihm zum Feste.
Er sieht sein Schätzel unten an
Mit weißen Tüchern angetan,
Die wend't sich —

erreiten: 'achieve by riding'. *Bindt's Pferd hauß an*: 'ties the horse outside' ('hauß' = 'draußen'). *Klafter*: 'fathoms'. *krapelt* (a variant of 'krabbelt'): 'scrambles'.

Written in 1774 and included in the 'Singspiel' *Claudine von Villa Bella*, a lighthearted melodrama of a maiden carried off to a brigands' lair (though the original was more intense and serious, in a 'Sturm und Drang' way). The ballad is sung by the brigand chief, Rugantino, who whispers to the maiden between the verses—all in all, then, not a ballad meant to be taken very seriously, as the roughness of the language and the zestful amusement with which the hideous terrors are listed also show. However, the language, rougher than that of any other of Goethe's ballads (note the syntax at the beginning of verse 2, the numerous abbreviations, the unusual vocabulary, and such hacked-out phrases as 'Bindt's Pferd hauß an'), show him writing in a 'popular' style, as he did also in the first version of 'Der König in Thule'. That there are not more poems in this style may be because its deliberate adoption could sound amusing or parodistic, as it does here.

The story breaks off because the brigand in the play is interrupted.

The roistering tone may be contrasted with the more 'Gothick' treatment of a similar story in Bürger's poem 'Lenore'.

VOR GERICHT

Von wem ich's habe, das sag' ich euch nicht,
Das Kind in meinem Leib.
Pfui, speit ihr aus, die Hure da!
Bin doch ein ehrlich Weib.

Mit wem ich mich traute, das sag' ich euch nicht,
Mein Schatz ist lieb und gut,
Trägt er eine goldne Kette am Hals,
Trägt er einen strohernen Hut.

Soll Spott und Hohn getragen sein,
Trag' ich allein den Hohn.
Ich kenn' ihn wohl, er kennt mich wohl,
Und Gott weiß auch davon.

Herr Pfarrer und Herr Amtmann ihr,
Ich bitt', laßt mich in Ruh!
Es ist mein Kind und bleibt mein Kind,
Ihr gebt mir ja nichts dazu.

Written about 1776. The last two lines of the second verse mean that the
lover is good whether he is rich or poor. The sturdy defiance of this mother
is in vivid contrast to the sentimentally treated women in the same situation,
drawn by Heinrich Wagner and G. A. Bürger, and indeed to Goethe's own
Gretchen in *Faust*. (Cp. *Wilhelm Meisters Theatralische Sendung*, II, vi, for
a closely similar situation.)

'FREUDVOLL UND LEIDVOLL'

'FREUDVOLL UND LEIDVOLL'

Goethe knew extremes of happiness and melancholia at first hand. We know from his autobiography that in the years when he was writing works as ecstatic as 'Mailied', as adventurous as *Götz* and as humorous as 'Lilis Park' he was also toying with ideas of suicide, as might be guessed from his authorship of *Werther*. His sadness has left comparatively little trace on his lyric verse: it was expressed rather in the opening monologue of *Faust*, in the novel, and in his letters. There are a few short poems, like the first three which follow, in which something of the violent changes of mood Goethe knew can be guessed. But, as so often, he preferred the 'dramatic' presentation in which he could live out a feeling without necessarily being wholly committed to it. 'Ich flüchtete mich hinter ein Bild', as he said on one occasion.

Goethe's novel *Wilhelm Meisters Lehrjahre* (published 1795, but begun in the late 1770's) contains a dozen or so poems, the best known of which are sung by a strange young girl, Mignon, and by a wandering Harper, who finally proves to be her father. Both are mysterious characters, coming more from the world of Ariosto or *The Faerie Queene* than from ordinary reality. Mignon is passionately devoted to Wilhelm Meister, despite her youth and the fact that she hovers uncertainly in her sex. She is called 'das Knabenmädchen', and in an earlier version of the novel, the *Theatralische Sendung*, which Goethe never revised for publication, she is referred to both as 'he' and 'she'. (Her very name is the masculine form of the French word meaning 'darling'.) She has great intuitive powers, and may represent in some way, without Goethe's ever having tried to formulate this to himself, the pristine, undivided unity at the very root of him, almost uncreate in its aloofness from the conflicts and contradictions of living. She may have been that part of him which knew best the paradisal region where he felt himself at one with Charlotte.

Certainly she expresses yearning in a way that Goethe never did in his straightforwardly lyrical poems.

The Harper, on the other hand, from whose marriage with his own sister Mignon was born, seems to be the reverse of all this, for he is close to madness from the beginning. In the same way, perhaps, that the mystic and the neurotic, the genius and the manic depressive, sometimes seem to display the same symptoms, so the intuitive Mignon is related to the almost insane Harper. In both there is intense loneliness. Mignon is lonely because, despite her closeness to Wilhelm, she knows her lack of real identity with him. The Harper, on the other hand, is excluded from Paradise because of his insight into the imperfection of things. He knows that the gods inflict guilt on men, and cannot forget it. Thus both Mignon, who is at the roots and seeks life (like the hermaphrodite Homunculus in *Faust*), and the Harper, who has life and abhors it, are equally in distress.

Both characters spring from Goethe's dim consciousness of the depths of his personality. He did fear madness at times, and was conscious of inexplicable powers of clairvoyance, telepathy, and prescience. By setting the poems in his novel he may have looked for some cathartic effect on himself, the shedding of yet further 'serpent-skins', as he often called his more obviously confessional works. The novel, however, makes a strange foil to these moving verses; Wilhelm treats the singers or speakers as though they were performing for his entertainment rather than pouring out their griefs, and even congratulates the Harper, who has been singing to himself, on stirring up his, Wilhelm's, feelings in so gratifying a way. One has the sense at times that Goethe later removed himself too far from the mood whence the poems had first sprung.

*　　*　　*

Freudvoll
Und leidvoll,
Gedankenvoll sein;
Langen

Und bangen
In schwebender Pein;
Himmelhoch jauchzend,
Zum Tode betrübt;
Glücklich allein
Ist die Seele, die liebt.

Klärchen's song from *Egmont* (written 1775–87), with which, she says, she lulled her lover to sleep. Set to music by Beethoven, Schubert and Liszt.

WANDRERS NACHTLIED

Der du von dem Himmel bist,
Alles Leid und Schmerzen stillest,
Den, der doppelt elend ist,
Doppelt mit Erquickung füllest,
Ach, ich bin des Treibens müde!
Was soll all der Schmerz und Lust?
Süßer Friede,
Komm, ach komm in meine Brust!

Written in 1776, a companion piece to 'Über allen Gipfeln' (p. 37 above) which is a kind of reply to it. Goethe said 'Nacht' where a modern German would say 'Abend'. An earlier version had in the second line 'Alle *Freud*' und Schmerzen', which brings the thought more into line with that of the poems here preceding and succeeding, as well as with the 'Schmerz und Lust' of line 6.

Alles geben die Götter, die unendlichen,
Ihren Lieblingen ganz,
Alle Freuden, die unendlichen,
Alle Schmerzen, die unendlichen, ganz.

Written in 1777, in a letter to Auguste Gräfin zu Stolberg, followed by the words: 'So sang ich neulich, als ich tief in einer herrlichen Mondnacht aus dem Flusse stieg, der vor meinem Garten durch die Wiesen fließt; und das bewahrheitet sich täglich an mir.' Never published by Goethe.

HARFENSPIELER

Wer sich der Einsamkeit ergibt,
Ach! der ist bald allein;
Ein jeder lebt, ein jeder liebt
Und läßt ihn seiner Pein.

Ja! laßt mich meiner Qual!
Und kann ich nur einmal
Recht einsam sein,
Dann bin ich nicht allein.

Es schleicht ein Liebender lauschend sacht,
Ob seine Freundin allein?
So überschleicht bei Tag und Nacht
Mich Einsamen die Pein,
Mich Einsamen die Qual.
Ach, werd ich erst einmal
Einsam im Grabe sein,
Da läßt sie mich allein!

Written before 1783. Some interpretations can mislead. It is not simply lonely people the Harper is singing about, but rather people who surrender to loneliness ('wer sich ... ergibt'). In fact the Harper, in his almost insane way, takes a perverse pleasure in being alone, welcoming it as though it were a lover fondling him, and there is a paradox in his longing for the *loneliness* of the grave. It is surprising, in the novel, to find Goethe continuing immediately after this with the remark that he cannot find words to express the charm of the conversation between Wilhelm and the old man. The poem is bleakly despairing, especially in the way the last line echoes on all the repetitions of 'Pein' and 'allein' that have gone before.

The 'Harfenspieler' songs are particularly well set to music by Hugo Wolf.

HARFENSPIELER

Wer nie sein Brot mit Tränen aß,
Wer nie die kummervollen Nächte
Auf seinem Bette weinend saß,
Der kennt euch nicht, ihr himmlischen Mächte.

Ihr führt ins Leben uns hinein,
Ihr laßt den Armen schuldig werden,
Dann überlaßt ihr ihn der Pein:
Denn alle Schuld rächt sich auf Erden.

Written not later than 1783. In the novel, the following verse is heard later by Wilhelm, separated from the two given here:

Ihm färbt der Morgensonne Licht
Den reinen Horizont mit Flammen,
Und über seinem schuld'gen Haupte bricht
Das schöne Bild der ganzen Welt zusammen.

Goethe published only the first verse of all with his poems as such, thus very much altering the sense (which was akin to that of 'Wonne der Wehmut'). With the second verse added (in the novel), the poem becomes bitter in its accusation against the gods. The third verse, added in a later version of the novel, begins to assert a detachment—the 'Armer' is spoken of in the third person, whereas 'uns' was used earlier, and there is a suggestion that the 'schöne Bild' remains, for those who are able to see it.

HARFENSPIELER

An die Türen will ich schleichen,
Still und sittsam will ich stehn;
Fromme Hand wird Nahrung reichen,
Und ich werde weitergehn.
Jeder wird sich glücklich scheinen,
Wenn mein Bild vor ihm erscheint;
Eine Träne wird er weinen,
Und ich weiß nicht, was er weint.

Written before 1795. Included only in the later version of the novel. The Harper is heard singing this verse shortly after he has set fire to a house in which Wilhelm was staying, and threatened the life of Wilhelm's son. The song 'enthielt den Trost eines Unglücklichen, der sich dem Wahnsinn ganz nahe fühlt'. The rather sing-song rhythm, the childlike reference to 'fromme Hand' (without the definite article), and the insouciant ending suit this state of mind, while the sequence of thoughts is unemphatically hideous—the stealthy approach to the door, the (assumed?) decorum, the automatic reception of a cold charity, the awareness of the donor's supposed secret rejoicing, and the final sense of complete ignorance and isolation.

MIGNON

Kennst du das Land, wo die Zitronen blühn,
Im dunkeln Laub die Gold-Orangen glühn,
Ein sanfter Wind vom blauen Himmel weht,
Die Myrte still und hoch der Lorbeer steht,
Kennst du es wohl?
Dahin! Dahin
Möcht ich mit dir, o mein Geliebter, ziehn.

Kennst du das Haus? Auf Säulen ruht sein Dach,
Es glänzt der Saal, es schimmert das Gemach,
Und Marmorbilder stehn und sehn mich an:
Was hat man dir, du armes Kind, getan?
Kennst du es wohl?
Dahin! Dahin
Möcht ich mit dir, o mein Beschützer, ziehn.

Kennst du den Berg und seinen Wolkensteg?
Das Maultier sucht im Nebel seinen Weg,
In Höhlen wohnt der Drachen alte Brut,
Es stürzt der Fels und über ihn die Flut;
Kennst du ihn wohl?
Dahin! Dahin
Geht unser Weg! o Vater, laß uns ziehn!

Written before 1783, appearing in both the earlier and the later versions of
the novel, where it is said that Mignon sang it to a zither, and in a foreign
language, the present version being but a poor translation of the original. 'Sie
fing jeden Vers [i.e. Strophe] feierlich und prächtig an, als ob sie auf etwas
Sonderbares aufmerksam machen, als ob sie etwas Wichtiges vortragen
wollte. Bei der dritten Zeile ward der Gesang dumpfer und düsterer;
das *Kennst du es wohl?* drückte sie geheimnisvoll und bedächtig aus; in
dem *Dahin! dahin* lag eine unwiderstehliche Sehnsucht, und ihr *laß uns
ziehn!* wußte sie bei jeder Wiederholung dergestalt zu modifizieren,
daß es bald bittend und dringend, bald treibend und vielversprechend war.'
Wilhelm correctly guesses the land to be Italy (the land of Goethe's own
longing), so that the mountains would seem to be the Alps, although the
perfect stillness and beauty suggest a paradisal country to be reached only
after tribulations and 'dragons'.

The sequence of sounds is incomparably rich: contrast the lines from Thomson's *Seasons*, which Goethe could have known:

> Bear me, Pomona, to thy citron groves,
> To where the lemon and the piercing lime,
> With the green orange glowing through the green,
> Their lighter glories blend.

With the opening question, Goethe establishes solemnity, where Thomson is concerned only with the happy thought of such a place. The pause after 'Land' suggests a slightly shorter one after 'Laub', 'Wind', and 'still', so that the verse seems continually hushed, though it sweetly moves forward again after each lilting hesitation. The repeated questions seem to become more urgent from verse to verse, while the broad vowel of the mysterious 'Vater', after the tighter vowels of 'Geliebter' and 'Beschützer', is like a cry of abandonment. (Originally Goethe had written 'o mein *Gebieter*!' in each verse.) The poem is full of such delicacies of sound. It has been set by Beethoven, Schubert, Schumann, Liszt and Wolf.

MIGNON

Nur wer die Sehnsucht kennt,
Weiß, was ich leide!
Allein und abgetrennt
Von aller Freude,
Seh ich ans Firmament
Nach jener Seite.
Ach! der mich liebt und kennt,
Ist in der Weite.
Es schwindelt mir, es brennt
Mein Eingeweide.
Nur wer die Sehnsucht kennt,
Weiß, was ich leide!

Written in 1785. In the later version of the novel Goethe wrote that it was sung by Mignon and the Harper 'als ein unregelmäßiges Duett mit dem herzlichsten [*sic*] Ausdruck'; in the earlier version it was sung by Mignon alone, when it naturally seemed to be an expression of yearning for Wilhelm. In the duet, since the Harper has no lover, and 'der' suggests a masculine one, the line 'der mich liebt und *kennt*' suggests a 'deus absconditus'. This helps to explain 'nach jener Seite', and the Biblical-sounding

'Eingeweide' ('bowels'), which may be a recollection from the Psalms. Perhaps, in a paradoxical way, Mignon yearns both for a mortal and for a heavenly lover. The repeated rhymes on certain sounds, as in 'Wer sich der Einsamkeit ergibt' (and Brentano's 'Der Spinnerin Lied'), release an agony of grief.

MIGNON

Heiß mich nicht reden, heiß mich schweigen,
Denn mein Geheimnis ist mir Pflicht;
Ich möchte dir mein ganzes Innre zeigen,
Allein das Schicksal will es nicht.

Zur rechten Zeit vertreibt der Sonne Lauf
Die finstre Nacht, und sie muß sich erhellen;
Der harte Fels schließt seinen Busen auf,
Mißgönnt der Erde nicht die tiefverborgnen Quellen.

Ein jeder sucht im Arm des Freundes Ruh,
Dort kann die Brust in Klagen sich ergießen;
Allein ein Schwur drückt mir die Lippen zu,
Und nur ein Gott vermag sie aufzuschließen.

Date of writing unknown, but included in both versions of the novel, each time in an entirely different context, and in neither case with a satisfying motivation, so that it makes the impression of having been rather more a poem that Goethe felt compelled to write than one which he conceived especially for the character of Mignon. (Might it have been meant originally for Charlotte von Stein's ears?) The intensity of the final line, and the enigmatic thought of lines 3 and 4 give the poem some distinction, but the ordinary imagery of verse 2, with its strange reversion to the alexandrine, and the conventionality of 'in Klagen sich ergießen' might have come from a less accomplished hand than Goethe's. It is almost as though the very awareness of something unrevealable had driven the poet into expressing himself in stock terms.

MIGNON

So laßt mich scheinen, bis ich werde;
Zieht mir das weiße Kleid nicht aus!
Ich eile von der schönen Erde
Hinab in jenes feste Haus.

Dort ruh ich eine kleine Stille,
Dann öffnet sich der frische Blick,
Ich lasse dann die reine Hülle,
Den Gürtel und den Kranz zurück.

Und jene himmlischen Gestalten,
Sie fragen nicht nach Mann und Weib,
Und keine Kleider, keine Falten
Umgeben den verklärten Leib.

Zwar lebt ich ohne Sorg und Mühe,
Doch fühlt ich tiefen Schmerz genung.
Vor Kummer altert ich zu frühe —
Macht mich auf ewig wieder jung!

Written in 1796 especially for the ending of *Wilhelm Meisters Lehrjahre*, in which Wilhelm goes to the house of his long-lost ideal love, the beautiful Natalie who once appeared to him as though in a vision (cp. 'Zueignung'), in search of Mignon. He is told Mignon is ill, and that recently, having been dressed in angel's clothes at a children's party, she begged to be allowed to go on wearing them till her death, which she expected very soon. These robes, then, are the 'weißes Kleid', and by 'so laßt mich scheinen' Mignon means that since she now seems an angel she would remain so till she becomes one in truth. Although the ideas seem rather close to the conventional sentiments of the time, and the metre is undistinguished, the phrase 'der frische Blick' is typically Goethean, and the vision of the naked, sexless body in the resurrection is his own. In allowing Mignon to die, Goethe was perhaps in part expressing his awareness that, at the time, he could not repeat the success of 'Kennst du das Land'.

ITALIAN JOURNEY

ITALIAN JOURNEY

The years 1786–8 were the most momentous in Goethe's life. Suddenly and clandestinely he left Karlsbad, where he was holidaying, on 3 September 1786 (the Duke's birthday, of all days) and made for Italy like a lover going to his mistress. His letters home, especially in the first few months, are full of high spirits: time and time again he speaks of being reborn and of returning a new man. He experiences 'eine innere Art von Verklärung..., ein Gefühl von freyerem Leben, höhere Existenz Leichtigkeit und Grazie'.

Moreover, he was agog with the feeling that at last he had unfathomed the deepest of Nature's secrets. It was as though he had penetrated to the heart of an ideal world in which, transfigured himself, he was at one with the pristine beauty of all creation, loving and understanding it all. In Italy he was close in spirit to the ancient world, the 'Urmenschen' of whom he knew from Homer (unlike Shakespeare here, Goethe saw them as ideals beyond all reproach); in Sicily the great wealth of flora tempted him to think he might come across the 'Urpflanze', which in its turn would have witnessed to the great unity of all living things, for its growth would have parallelled the spiritual growth of men. Goethe was filled with the sense of being caught up in the vast rhythmic flow of Nature, like a Faust at last capable of sharing in the life of the Earth-Spirit, and he exulted at the fitness of all that happened: 'was ist doch ein Lebendiges für ein köstliches, herrliches Ding! wie abgemessen zu seinem Zustande, *wie wahr, wie seiend!*' (my italics). He was at the growing-point of life, opening up like a bud.

Goethe wrote little poetry at this time, though he revised and added to plays already begun and gathered data for his scientific papers. The famous work of poetry relating to these years, the *Römische Elegien* (containing twenty elegies in all), was written after his return, from the autumn of 1788 to the spring of 1790, a time when he was living not with an Italian

mistress but with Christiane Vulpius, by whom he had many children and whom, in 1806, he married.

Like many of the poems which Goethe wrote for the next twenty years—the epic *Hermann und Dorothea*, the poems entitled *Metamorphose der Pflanzen*, *Amor als Landschaftsmaler*, the *Venezianische Epigramme*, the *Xenien*, and so on, the *Elegies* are in classical metre, in elegiac couplets. Their themes are not mournful, any more than are the elegiac poets whom Goethe emulated, Catullus, Tibullus, and Propertius; on the contrary they celebrate erotic delights with a freedom such as Goethe had never used before, even in his Anacreontic days, and which is astonishing when one thinks that he was idealizing the almost sexless Iphigenie at this time. Not that Goethe intended to shock. As he said to Eckermann much later, 'Es liegen in den verschiedenen poetischen Formen geheimnisvolle große Wirkungen. Wenn man den Inhalt meiner *Römischen Elegien* in den Ton und die Versart von Byrons *Don Juan* übertragen wollte, so müßte sich das Ganze ganz verrucht ausnehmen.' The *Erotica Romana*, as Goethe originally called them, were to be noble celebrations of bodily pleasures, not naughty peepshows. They were one expression of his realization in Italy that all things are and work for good.

The classical form had disadvantages. The hexameter and the pentameter were made originally by people who reckoned their verse by the length of syllables, the 'quantity', rather than by the stress, as Germans do. The hexameter requires six feet, of which the first four may be spondees or dactyls (′ ′ or ′ x x), the fifth must be a dactyl, the sixth a spondee or trochee, and spondees are not easy to find in German. The pentameter, being as a rule mostly dactylic, is a simpler matter. Schiller's famous paradigm is often used as a mnemonic:

$$\text{Im Hex|ameter | steigt : des | Springquells | flüssige | Säule}$$
$$\text{Im Pent|ameter | drauf : fällt er mel|odisch her|ab.}$$

What usually happens in practice is that instead of spondees there are trochees—as in the word 'Säule' above—and that the

line tends to become a sequence of trochees interspersed with dactyls, the two short syllables in the latter equalling in length the one short syllable in the trochee. Or else the natural accent is distorted, as it is in Schiller's lines. Nobody who did not have the hexameter rhythm already in mind would say 'Im Hexameter'; he would say 'Im Hexameter'. The poet Voss, a contemporary of Goethe's who translated Homer, satirized the classical verse of both Goethe and Schiller in the lines

In Wei|mar und in|Jena ⁝ macht man | Hex|ameter | wie der, [i.e. wie dieser]

Aber die | Pentamet|er ⁝ sind doch noch | exzellent|er.|

and Voss's exaggeration does bring out Goethe's occasional negligence in matters of prosody. (He was, writes Gilbert Highet in *The Classical Tradition*, 'much too lax in using a difficult metre. ... There are many lines in Goethe's elegies which only classical scholars can read with understanding, and no classical scholar can read with pleasure' (pp. 381–2).) In the Third Elegy, printed below (p. 129), he requires an unnatural stress on 'und' in lines 4 and 16, as well as on 'lauten' in line 13 (which he makes a spondee) and in line 14 on 'sich'; one would not emphasize 'du' in the first line but for the requirement of the metre. It is generous to say, as one critic does, that Goethe 'cared more for truth and force of expression than for correctness of technique', but the one is sometimes an aspect of the other. A reader has to experiment a good deal to find out how to read such a line as this:

Besser ist ihr Tisch nun bestellt: es fehlet an Kleidern...

which seems to run naturally like this

but which evidently has to be read like this

The question of classical metres was hotly argued in Goethe's time (see C. H. Trevelyan, *Goethe and the Greeks*, Cambridge, 1941, Appendix); today they have become part of an accepted tradition, if no longer a living one.

✳ ✳ ✳

Saget, Steine, mir an, o sprecht, ihr hohen Paläste!
Straßen, redet ein Wort! Genius,* regst du dich nicht?
Ja, es ist alles beseelt in deinen heiligen Mauern,
Ewige Roma; nur mir schweiget noch alles so still.
O wer flüstert mir zu, an welchem Fenster erblick ich
Einst das holde Geschöpf, das mich versengend erquickt?
Ahn ich die Wege noch nicht, durch die ich immer und immer,
Zu ihr und von ihr zu gehn, opfre die köstliche Zeit?
Noch betracht ich Kirch und Palast, Ruinen und Säulen,
Wie ein bedächtiger Mann schicklich die Reise benutzt.
Doch bald ist es vorbei; dann wird ein einziger Tempel,
Amors Tempel, nur sein, der den Geweihten empfängt.
Eine Welt zwar bist du, o Rom; doch ohne die Liebe
Wäre die Welt nicht die Welt, wäre denn Rom auch nicht
Rom.

Genius: 'genius loci', the spirit of the place, not 'genius' in the 'Sturm und Drang' sense.

This is the first Elegy, and from the beginning can be felt what the Romantic critic Friedrich Schlegel called 'hie und da ein Anhauch von Parodie, ein leiser komischer Anstrich', natural enough, as he says, in one who is intentionally putting on the mask of an ancient Roman. There is a touch of the old 'Sturm und Drang' humour in 'versengend erquickt', even though the girl is now only a 'holdes Geschöpf'. Goethe smiles at his own tourist-like attitude, but he is genuinely moved by the 'hohe Paläste', the 'heilige Mauern'. The final couplet is disappointing as wit, and contorted in its rhythm, which places a false stress on 'Eine' and removes the natural stresses on 'zwar' and 'nicht', yet the good humour of the poem comes through all the same.

Herbstlich leuchtet die Flamme vom ländlich geselligen Herde,
Knistert und glänzet, wie rasch! sausend vom Reisig empor.
Diesen Abend erfreut sie mich mehr; denn eh noch zur Kohle
Sich das Bündel verzehrt, unter die Asche sich neigt,
Kommt mein liebliches Mädchen. Dann flammen Reisig und
Scheite,
Und die erwärmete Nacht wird uns ein glänzendes Fest.

Morgen frühe geschäftig verläßt sie das Lager der Liebe,
 Weckt aus der Asche behend Flammen aufs neue hervor.
Denn vor andern verlieh der Schmeichlerin Amor die Gabe,
 Freude zu wecken, die kaum still wie zu Asche versank.

The ninth elegy. Amor is the subject of the last couplet (which Goethe
could have had in mind when he spoke of how scandalous his themes
would have sounded in Byron's treatment), 'der Schmeichlerin' being
dative. Throughout, the flame is a symbol of love-making.
The exclamation mark in line 2 does not mark the end of a sentence.

Laß dich, Geliebte, nicht reun, daß du mir so schnell dich
 ergeben!
 Glaub es, ich denke nicht frech, denke nicht niedrig von dir.
Vielfach wirken die Pfeile des Amor: einige ritzen,
 Und vom schleichenden Gift kranket auf Jahre das Herz.
Aber mächtig befiedert, mit frisch geschliffener Schärfe
 Dringen die andern ins Mark, zünden behende das Blut.
In der heroischen Zeit, da Götter und Göttinnen liebten,
 Folgte Begierde dem Blick, folgte Genuß der Begier.
Glaubst du, es habe sich lange die Göttin der Liebe besonnen,
 Als im Idäischen Hain einst ihr Anchises* gefiel?
Hätte Luna gesäumt, den schönen Schläfer* zu küssen,
 O, so hätt ihn geschwind, neidend, Aurora geweckt.
Hero* erblickte Leandern* am lauten Fest, und behende
 Stürzte der Liebende sich heiß in die nächtliche Flut.
Rhea Sylvia* wandelt, die fürstliche* Jungfrau, der Tiber
 Wasser zu schöpfen, hinab, und sie ergreifet der Gott.
So erzeugte die Söhne sich Mars! — Die Zwillinge tränket
 Eine Wölfin, und Rom nennt sich die Fürstin* der Welt.

Anchises: the father of Aeneas (ancestor of the Roman nation, in Vergil's epic), whom
he begot by Venus. *den schönen Schläfer*: Endymion. *Leander* was drowned in the
Hellespont, swimming to his lover, *Hero* of Sestos. *Rhea Sylvia*, a vestal virgin, was
raped by Mars. The twins she bore, Romulus and Remus, were suckled by a wolf
and founded the city of Rome. *Fürstlich* herself, she thus gave rise to a greater
Fürstin.

The poet comforts his mistress, who has yielded to him quickly, saying that he does not think ill of her for that. The Roman gods and goddesses took their lovers instantly. The barbaric example of Mars and the brisk tone of the narration at this point, however, do not consort well with the love of the mortals Hero and Leander for one another: the Greek dramatists would have given Mars short shrift. The classical references only help to stress the poet's self-consciousness (if he is really at ease he has no need of these historic buttresses) and in a certain degree his condescension. The effect is more pleasing when the examples refer to instantaneous passion, rather than satyr-like lust. (Cp. the note on p. 164.)

Cupido, loser,* eigensinniger Knabe!
Du batst mich um Quartier auf einige Stunden.
Wie viele Tag' und Nächte bist du geblieben!
Und bist nun herrisch und Meister im Hause geworden!

Von meinem breiten Lager bin ich vertrieben;
Nun sitz ich an der Erde, Nächte gequälet;
Dein Mutwill schüret Flamm auf Flamme des Herdes,
Verbrennet den Vorrat des Winters und senget mich Armen.

Du hast mir mein Geräte* verstellt und verschoben;
Ich such und bin wie blind und irre geworden.
Du lärmst so ungeschickt; ich fürchte, das Seelchen
Entflieht, um dir zu entfliehn, und räumet die Hütte.

<div align="center">

loser: 'mischievous'. *Geräte*: 'furniture'.

</div>

Written in Rome in 1787 or 1788, this is in a freer metre than the *Elegies*, and has more liveliness. The humour Schlegel found in the *Elegies* is also clearly in evidence. One hears a human voice, exasperated, fuming with mock rage, and at last genuinely concerned at the lengths to which love can go—a theme of Goethe's love-poems from early days.

COPHTISCHES* LIED

Lasset Gelehrte sich zanken und streiten,
Streng und bedächtig die Lehrer auch sein!
Alle die Weisesten aller der Zeiten
Lächeln und winken und stimmen mit ein:

Töricht,* auf Beßrung der Toren zu harren!
Kinder der Klugheit, o habet die Narren
Eben zum Narren auch, wie sichs gehört!

Merlin der Alte, im leuchtenden Grabe,
Wo ich als Jüngling gesprochen ihn habe,
Hat mich mit ähnlicher Antwort belehrt:
Töricht, auf Beßrung der Toren zu harren!
Kinder der Klugheit, o habet die Narren
Eben zum Narren auch, wie sichs gehört!

Und auf den Höhen der indischen Lüfte
Und in den Tiefen ägyptischer Grüfte
Hab ich das heilige Wort nur gehört:
Töricht, auf Beßrung der Toren zu harren!
Kinder der Klugheit, o habet die Narren
Eben zum Narren auch, wie sichs gehört!

Cophtisches: 'Coptic'. The Grand Copt was the supposed founder of Egyptian Free-masonry. In Goethe's comedy *Der Groß-Cophta* (1791), which does not include this song, the mountebank Cagliostro claims to be the emissary of the Grand Copt. *Töricht*: understand 'es ist töricht'.

EIN ANDERES*

Geh! gehorche meinen Winken,
Nutze deine jungen Tage,
Lerne zeitig klüger sein:
Auf des Glückes großer Waage
Steht die Zunge selten ein;*
Du mußt steigen oder sinken,
Du mußt herrschen und gewinnen,
Oder dienen und verlieren,
Leiden oder triumphieren,
Amboß oder Hammer sein.

Ein anderes: 'anderes' here means 'second', i.e. 'a second Coptic song'. *Steht...ein*: 'the pointer (on the scales) seldom stands still'.

Written between 1787 and 1789, these songs were meant for an opera libretto on the subject of Cagliostro; Goethe used much of his material instead for the prose play *Der Groß-Cophta*. Hugo Wolf's setting of the first is both savagely threatening and lugubrious; the piano imitates between verses the shaking of a jester's cap and bells, capturing the strange, zany seriousness of the words. Fools are meant to be fooled—Goethe was not unconvinced of this, though, as so often, he speaks here in an adopted character. The idea was a sardonic aspect of his whole Italian experience of the fitness of things.

The second Coptic song is also set most sensitively by Wolf, affecting compassion in lines 2 and 3, swelling imperiously, and hurling the last words defiantly into a grandiose, stately march which ends in discord. The choice to be made between being an anvil and a hammer is not left open to doubt. (Compare 'Der Winter und Timur' and 'Laß dich, Geliebte, nicht reun' on pp. 144 and 129. The moral drawn has some relationship to the anti-Christian mood expressed in 'Die Braut von Korinth' and other poems.)

LATER NARRATIVE POEMS
AND BALLADS

LATER NARRATIVE POEMS
AND BALLADS

The chief gain Goethe had from the Italian Journey of 1786–8 was the sense that all things were approvable: a sense he had had before, but never so strongly. He took in now not only the Italian world, the world of Rome, ancient and modern, the world of Greece, but also that of the Orient. Within a few years Goethe was writing in imitation of, or borrowing material from, Sanskrit, Indian, Persian and Chinese sources; he was publishing works on optics, botany, meteorology, geology, anatomy, painting, sculpture and architecture (as well as writing lyrics, novels, epic poems, plays, directing the theatre for many years, and being in effect prime minister of Weimar). More than ever before he had the sense of riding on the crest of the wave of his times, almost of being their representative.

This 'all-embracing' mood was not only cultural but affected his personal life. Italy had released him from sexual constraints and he was now on the road to seeing everything in life as welcome, nothing as condemnable. For this reason he turned more explicitly against Christian teaching than he had done hitherto, and, although he continued to speak reverently of Christ, denounced all that part of Christianity which seemed to him life-denying. This is the theme of the poem 'Groß ist die Diana der Epheser', printed below, of 'Die Braut von Korinth', in which a dead, Christian bride plays the part of a vampire, preying on the living, and of 'Die erste Walpurgisnacht', in which Christians are frightened away by pagans who pretend to be horrifying demons of the kind Christians expect to see— 'those who believe wickedness exists will naturally see such monsters at the slightest pretext' is the implied moral. (By contrast, 'Die Legende vom Hufeisen' presents a more sympathetic picture.) Other narrative poems, on the other hand, celebrate sexual love, as does 'Der Gott und die Bajadere',

or, what is equivalent, deliberately include the outcast, the rejected member of society, as does 'Paria' (both below). In the brave new world now opening for Goethe there is nothing that is not appropriate. 'Wie wahr, wie seiend' he had exclaimed in Italy, and so it remained. Where naturalness led to ferocity, as it did in 'Der Winter und Timur', this too was met by forces adequate, within the natural order of things, for its suppression. The ruthless Timur (Tamburlaine) was met by an equally ruthless winter, the man empowered like a god was put down by no less a power. In the words Goethe used as the motto to the twentieth book of his autobiography, 'Nemo contra deum nisi deus ipse': 'None against God save God Himself' or 'None against God unless himself a god'.

Many of the ballads and narrative poems written after the return from Italy thus have a more deliberate purpose than those of the earlier period. They are meant to impart Goethe's new sense of acceptance—and indeed some of them were written during the so-called 'Balladenjahr' of 1797 when Goethe and Schiller combined to spread their cultural message among a wider public. At the same time, there is something more formal about them than there is in the ballads of before 1786. Many are in the same metre (trochaic tetrameters) as that which established itself once before for a short while in 'Mahomets-Gesang'. As a rule, however, this is a metre rather than a rhythm—Goethe selects his metre and adheres to it closely, occasionally with a characteristic effect, as in the refrains of 'Der Gott und die Bajadere' and 'Der Zauberlehrling', but generally with more regard to the steady beat than to the quantities of the words. On the whole he is for a while more interested in sense than in sound.

* * *

DER GOTT UND DIE BAJADERE*

INDISCHE LEGENDE

Mahadöh, der Herr der Erde,
Kommt herab zum sechsten Mal,

Daß er unsersgleichen werde,
Mit zu fühlen Freud und Qual.
Er bequemt sich, hier zu wohnen,
Läßt sich alles selbst geschehn.
Soll er strafen oder schonen,
Muß er Menschen menschlich sehn.
Und hat er die Stadt sich als Wandrer betrachtet,
Die Großen belauert, auf Kleine geachtet,
Verläßt er sie abends, um weiter zu gehn.

Als er nun hinausgegangen,
Wo die letzten Häuser sind,
Sieht er, mit gemalten Wangen,
Ein verlornes schönes Kind.
Grüß dich, Jungfrau! — Dank der Ehre!
Wart, ich komme gleich hinaus —
Und wer bist du? — Bajadere,
Und dies ist der Liebe Haus.
Sie rührt sich, die Zimbeln zum Tanze zu schlagen,
Sie weiß sich so lieblich im Kreise zu tragen,
Sie neigt sich und biegt sich, und reicht ihm den Strauß.

Schmeichelnd zieht sie ihn zur Schwelle,
Lebhaft ihn ins Haus hinein.
Schöner Fremdling, lampenhelle
Soll sogleich die Hütte sein.
Bist du müd, ich will dich laben,
Lindern deiner Füße Schmerz.
Was du willst, das sollst du haben,
Ruhe, Freuden oder Scherz.
Sie lindert geschäftig geheuchelte Leiden.
Der Göttliche lächelt; er siehet mit Freuden
Durch tiefes Verderben ein menschliches Herz.

Und er fordert Sklavendienste;
Immer heitrer wird sie nur,
Und des Mädchens frühe Künste*
Werden nach und nach Natur.

137

Und so stellet auf die Blüte
Bald und bald die Frucht sich ein;
Ist Gehorsam im Gemüte,
Wird nicht fern die Liebe sein.
Aber, sie schärfer und schärfer zu prüfen,
Wählet der Kenner der Höhen und Tiefen
Lust und Entsetzen und grimmige Pein.

Und er küßt die bunten Wangen,
Und sie fühlt der Liebe Qual,
Und das Mädchen steht gefangen,
Und sie weint zum erstenmal;
Sinkt zu seinen Füßen nieder,
Nicht um Wollust noch Gewinst,
Ach! und die gelenken Glieder,
Sie versagen allen Dienst.
Und so zu des Lagers vergnüglicher Feier
Bereiten den dunklen behaglichen Schleier
Die nächtlichen Stunden, das schöne Gespinst.

Spät entschlummert unter Scherzen,
Früh erwacht nach kurzer Rast,
Findet sie an ihrem Herzen
Tot den vielgeliebten Gast.
Schreiend stürzt sie auf ihn nieder,
Aber nicht erweckt sie ihn;
Und man trägt die starren Glieder
Bald zur Flammengrube* hin.
Sie höret die Priester, die Totengesänge,
Sie raset und rennet und teilet die Menge.
Wer bist du? was drängt zu der Grube dich hin?

Bei der Bahre stürzt sie nieder,
Ihr Geschrei durchdringt die Luft:
Meinen Gatten will ich wieder!
Und ich such ihn in der Gruft.
Soll zu Asche mir zerfallen
Dieser Glieder Götterpracht?

Mein! er war es, mein vor allen!
Ach, nur Eine süße Nacht!
Es singen die Priester: Wir tragen die Alten,
Nach langem Ermatten und spätem Erkalten,
Wir tragen die Jugend, noch eh sies gedacht.

Höre deiner Priester Lehre:
Dieser war dein Gatte nicht.
Lebst du doch als Bajadere,
Und so hast du keine Pflicht.
Nur dem Körper folgt der Schatten
In das stille Totenreich;
Nur die Gattin folgt dem Gatten:
Das ist Pflicht und Ruhm zugleich.
Ertöne, Drommete,* zu heiliger Klage!
O nehmet, ihr Götter! die Zierde der Tage,
O nehmet den Jüngling in Flammen zu euch!

So das Chor, das ohn Erbarmen
Mehret ihres Herzens Not;
Und mit ausgestreckten Armen
Springt sie in den heißen Tod.
Doch der Götter-Jüngling hebet
Aus der Flamme sich empor,
Und in seinen Armen schwebet
Die Geliebte mit hervor.
Es freut sich die Gottheit der reuigen Sünder;
Unsterbliche heben verlorene Kinder
Mit feurigen Armen zum Himmel empor.

Bajadere: 'courtesan'. *frühe Künste*: viz. 'initial artificiality'. *Flammengrube*: the trench in which the body is to be cremated. *Drommete*: 'Trompete'.

Written in June 1797, this poem teaches (like *Paria*) that sexual desire can be worthy in the sight of the gods. The bayadere or courtesan is at first merely a paid servant who assumes the expressions of love most calculated to please her client. The god sees, through such 'tiefes Verderben', the possibility of true love growing and encourages this in the girl, first by pretending to sufferings which as a god he cannot truly feel, then by

demanding of her the services of a slave, which involve for her not only pleasures but also grim torments, requiring her obedience (verse 4 seems to present the god as a sadist). Obedience, rather than the repentance spoken of in the last verse, is the chief quality leading to the love she feels, and there is an old-fashioned Oriental quality about it, leading at last to her insistence on her right to die on the funeral pyre, as wives commonly did in the now suppressed rite of suttee. These comparatively barbaric features tinge the portrayal of the god's delight in true, self-sacrificing love, and of his mercy towards those whom the orthodox easily despise. Goethe's message, however, was mainly concerned with the idea of 'Flammentod', as in 'Selige Sehnsucht' (p. 156 below).

The trochaic tetrameters, having masculine rhymes in alternate lines, give a more reposeful effect than those of 'Der Zauberling', with its entirely feminine rhymes. The refrain is most suited to the sinuous dance of the bayadere in v. 2.

DER ZAUBERLEHRLING

Hat der alte Hexenmeister
Sich doch einmal wegbegeben!
Und nun sollen seine Geister
Auch nach meinem Willen leben.
Seine Wort' und Werke
Merkt ich und den Brauch,
Und mit Geistesstärke
Tu ich Wunder auch.

Walle! walle
Manche Strecke,
Daß, zum Zwecke,
Wasser fließe
Und mit reichem, vollem Schwalle
Zu dem Bade sich ergieße.

Und nun komm, du alter Besen!
Nimm die schlechten Lumpenhüllen;
Bist schon lange Knecht gewesen:
Nun erfülle meinen Willen!

Auf zwei Beinen stehe,
Oben sei ein Kopf,
Eile nun und gehe
Mit dem Wassertopf!

Walle! walle
Manche Strecke,
Daß, zum Zwecke,
Wasser fließe
Und mit reichem, vollem Schwalle
Zu dem Bade sich ergieße.

Seht, er läuft zum Ufer nieder,
Wahrlich! ist schon an dem Flusse,
Und mit Blitzesschnelle wieder
Ist er hier mit raschem Gusse.
Schon zum zweiten Male!
Wie das Becken schwillt!
Wie sich jede Schale
Voll mit Wasser füllt!

Stehe! stehe!
Denn wir haben
Deiner Gaben
Vollgemessen!* —
Ach, ich merk es! Wehe! wehe!
Hab ich doch das Wort vergessen!

Ach, das Wort, worauf am Ende
Er das wird, was er gewesen.
Ach, er läuft und bringt behende!
Wärst du doch der alte Besen!
Immer neue Güsse
Bringt er schnell herein,
Ach! und hundert Flüsse
Stürzen auf mich ein.

Nein, nicht länger
Kann ichs lassen;

Will ihn fassen.
Das ist Tücke!
Ach! nun wird mir immer bänger!
Welche Miene! welche Blicke!

O, du Ausgeburt der Hölle!
Soll das ganze Haus ersaufen?
Seh ich über jede Schwelle
Doch schon Wasserströme laufen.
Ein verruchter Besen,
Der nicht hören will!
Stock, der du gewesen,
Steh doch wieder still!

Willsts am Ende
Gar nicht lassen?
Will dich fassen,
Will dich halten
Und das alte Holz behende
Mit dem scharfen Beile spalten.

Seht, da kommt er schleppend wieder!
Wie ich mich nur auf dich werfe,
Gleich, o Kobold, liegst du nieder;
Krachend trifft die glatte Schärfe.
Wahrlich! brav getroffen!
Seht, er ist entzwei!
Und nun kann ich hoffen,
Und ich atme frei!

Wehe! wehe!
Beide Teile
Stehn in Eile
Schon als Knechte
Völlig fertig in die Höhe!
Helft mir, ach! ihr hohen Mächte!

Und sie laufen! Naß und nässer
Wirds im Saal und auf den Stufen.

Welch entsetzliches Gewässer!
Herr und Meister! hör mich rufen! —
Ach, da kommt der Meister!
Herr, die Not ist groß!
Die ich rief, die Geister
Werd ich nun nicht los.

'In die Ecke,
Besen! Besen!
Seids gewesen.*
Denn als Geister
Ruft euch nur, zu diesem Zwecke,
Erst hervor der alte Meister.'*

Denn wir haben...vollgemessen: i.e. 'we have enjoyed the gifts you bring in full measure'. *Seids gewesen:* i.e. 'consider all that as over and done with'. *der alte Meister:* the wizard himself, who speaks the final verse.

Written in 1797 and based on an old legend, this resembles many of the later ballads in having a didactic element. The words 'Die ich rief, die Geister, werd ich nun nicht los' are often used proverbially. *L'Apprenti Sorcier* by Dukas realizes the same story, more eerily, in music.

GROSS IST DIE DIANA DER EPHESER

APOSTELGESCHICHTE 19, 39

Zu Ephesus ein Goldschmied saß
In seiner Werkstatt, pochte,
So gut er konnt, ohn Unterlaß,
So zierlich ers vermochte.
Als Knab und Jüngling kniet' er schon
Im Tempel vor der Göttin Thron
Und hatte den Gürtel unter den Brüsten,
Worin so manche Tiere nisten,
Zu Hause treulich nachgefeilt,
Wie's ihm der Vater zugeteilt;
Und leitete sein kunstreich Streben
In frommer Wirkung durch das Leben.

Da hört er denn auf einmal laut
Eines Gassenvolkes Windesbraut, *
Als gäbs einen Gott so im Gehirn,
Da! hinter des Menschen alberner Stirn,
Der sei viel herrlicher als das Wesen,
An dem wir die Breite der Gottheit lesen.

Der alte Künstler horcht nur auf,
Läßt seinen Knaben auf den Markt den Lauf,
Feilt immer fort an Hirschen und Tieren,
Die seiner Gottheit Kniee zieren,
Und hofft, es könnte das Glück ihm walten,
Ihr Angesicht würdig zu gestalten.

*

Wills aber einer anders halten,
So mag er nach Belieben schalten;
Nur soll er nicht das Handwerk schänden,
Sonst wird er schlecht und schmählich enden.

Windesbraut: 'whirlwind'; i.e. 'whirling' voices.

Written in 1812, this is more of an anti-Christian parable than a ballad, although the jocular tone and jaunty rhythms of the 'Knittelverse' preclude any sermonizing. The sub-title should perhaps read Acts xix. 28.

In the story in The Acts of the Apostles, to which Goethe refers in his title, a goldsmith complains that the apostles' teaching, according to which gods made by hands are not gods at all, will deprive him of his livelihood as an image-maker, whereupon he instigates an uproar. Goethe's goldsmith is both more peaceable and more confident, reflecting Goethe's own conviction that concrete realities are more valuable than intellectual or abstract concepts, such as the Christian God is here taken to be. Compare the use of 'Knittelverse' to convey homely sincerity in 'Rezensent' on p. 77 above.

DER WINTER UND TIMUR*

So umgab sie nun der Winter
Mit gewalt'gem Grimme. Streuend
Seinen Eishauch zwischen alle,

Hetzt' er die verschiednen Winde
Widerwärtig auf sie ein.
Über sie gab er Gewaltkraft
Seinen frostgespitzten Stürmen,
Stieg in Timurs Rat hernieder,
Schrie ihn drohend an und sprach so:
'Leise, langsam, Unglücksel'ger,
Wandle, du Tyrann des Unrechts;
Sollen länger noch die Herzen
Sengen, brennen deinen* Flammen?
Bist du der verdammten Geister
Einer, wohl! ich bin der andre.
Du bist Greis, ich auch, erstarren
Machen wir so Land als Menschen.
Mars! du bist's! ich bin Saturnus,
Übeltätige Gestirne,
Im Verein* die schrecklichsten.
Tötest du die Seele, kältest
Du den Luftkreis: meine Lüfte
Sind noch kälter, als du sein kannst.
Quälen deine wilden Heere
Gläubige mit tausend Martern:
Wohl, in meinen Tagen soll sich,
Geb' es Gott! was Schlimmres finden.
Und bei Gott, dir schenk' ich nichts.*
Hör' es Gott, was ich dir biete!
Ja bei Gott! von Todeskälte
Nicht, o Greis, verteid'gen soll dich
Breite Kohlenglut vom Herde,
Keine Flamme des Dezembers.'

Timur: Tamburlaine, the Mongol conqueror (1336–1405). *deinen*: the sense is 'shall people burn *in* or *because of* your flames?' *Im Verein*: astrologically the planets Mars and Saturn portend evil when 'in conjunction'. *dir schenk' ich nichts*: 'I will have no mercy on you'.

Written in December 1814, this is closely modelled on a Latin translation of an old Arabic poem expressing hatred of the ferocious tyrant Tamburlaine. It is included in Goethe's collection of poems in the Persian manner,

West-östlicher Divan, where it is associated with a love-poem whence it takes a special sense (see p. 158 below). The powerful thrust of the poem, the savagery of its denunciation, is an expression of that amoral *daimon* to which Goethe refers in book 20 of his autobiography and in conversations with Eckermann. It is also in part a reflection on Napoleon and the Moscow campaign of 1812, for Napoleon was in Goethe's eyes an elemental being, to be subdued only by a power in the universe of a stature equal to his own, rather than by Blücher or the Duke of Wellington.

PARIA*

DES PARIA GEBET

Großer Brahma,* Herr der Mächte!
Alles ist von deinem Samen,
Und so bist du der Gerechte!
Hast du denn allein die Brahmen,*
Nur die Rajahs und die Reichen,
Hast du sie allein geschaffen?
Oder bist auch dus, der Affen
Werden ließ und unseresgleichen?

Edel sind wir nicht zu nennen:
Denn das Schlechte, das gehört uns,
Und was andre tödlich kennen,
Das alleine, das vermehrt uns.
Mag dies für die Menschen gelten,
Mögen sie uns doch verachten;
Aber du, du sollst uns achten,
Denn du könntest alle schelten.

Also, Herr, nach diesem Flehen,
Segne mich zu deinem Kinde;
Oder eines laß entstehen,
Das auch mich mit dir verbinde!
Denn du hast den Bajaderen*
Eine Göttin selbst erhoben;
Auch wir andern, dich zu loben,
Wollen solch ein Wunder hören.

LEGENDE

Wasser holen geht die reine,
Schöne Frau des hohen Brahmen,
Des verehrten, fehlerlosen,
Ernstester Gerechtigkeit.
Täglich von dem heiligen Flusse
Holt sie köstlichstes Erquicken —
Aber wo ist Krug und Eimer?
Sie bedarf derselben nicht.
Seligem Herzen, frommen Händen
Ballt sich die bewegte Welle
Herrlich zu kristallner Kugel;
Diese trägt sie, frohen Busens,
Reiner Sitte, holden Wandelns,
Vor den Gatten in das Haus.

Heute kommt die morgendliche
Im Gebet zu Ganges' Fluten,
Beugt sich zu der klaren Fläche —
Plötzlich überraschend spiegelt,
Aus des höchsten Himmels Breiten
Über ihr vorübereilend,
Allerlieblichste Gestalt
Hehren Jünglings, den des Gottes
Uranfänglich schönes Denken
Aus dem ewgen Busen schuf.
Solchen schauend, fühlt ergriffen
Von verwirrenden Gefühlen
Sie das innere tiefste Leben,
Will verharren in dem Anschaun,
Weist es weg, da kehrt es wieder,
Und verworren strebt sie flutwärts,
Mit unsichrer Hand zu schöpfen;
Aber ach! sie schöpft nicht mehr!
Denn des Wassers heilige Welle
Scheint zu fliehn, sich zu entfernen,

10-2

Sie erblickt nur hohler Wirbel*
Grause Tiefen unter sich.

Arme sinken, Tritte straucheln,
Ists denn auch der Pfad nach Hause?
Soll sie zaudern? soll sie fliehen?
Will sie denken, wo Gedanke,
Rat und Hilfe gleich versagt? —
Und so tritt sie vor den Gatten;
Er erblickt sie, Blick ist Urteil,
Hohen Sinns ergreift das Schwert er,
Schleppt sie zu dem Totenhügel,
Wo Verbrecher büßend bluten.
Wüßte sie zu widerstreben?
Wüßte sie sich zu entschuldgen,
Schuldig, keiner Schuld bewußt?

Und er kehrt mit blutigem Schwerte
Sinnend zu der stillen Wohnung;
Da entgegnet ihm der Sohn.
'Wessen Blut ists? Vater! Vater!' —
Der Verbrecherin! — 'Mitnichten!
Denn es starret nicht am Schwerte
Wie verbrecherische Tropfen,
Fließt wie aus der Wunde frisch.
Mutter, Mutter! tritt heraus her!
Ungerecht war nie der Vater,
Sage, was er jetzt verübt.' —
Schweige! Schweige! 's ist das ihre! —
'Wessen ist es?' — Schweige! Schweige!
'Wäre meiner Mutter Blut!!!
Was geschehen? was verschuldet?
Her das Schwert! ergriffen hab ichs;
Deine Gattin magst du töten,
Aber meine Mutter nicht!
In die Flammen* folgt die Gattin
Ihrem einzig Angetrauten,

148

Seiner einzig teuren Mutter
In das Schwert der treue Sohn.'

Halt, o halte! rief der Vater,
Noch ist Raum, enteil, enteile!
Füge Haupt dem Rumpfe wieder,
Du berührest mit dem Schwerte,
Und lebendig folgt sie dir.

Eilend, atemlos erblickt er
Staunend zweier Frauen Körper
Überkreuzt, und so die Häupter —
Welch Entsetzen! welche Wahl!
Dann der Mutter Haupt erfaßt er,
Küßt es nicht, das tot erblaßte;
Auf des nächsten Rumpfes Lücke
Setzt ers eilig, mit dem Schwerte
Segnet er das fromme Werk.

Aufersteht ein Riesenbildnis. —
Von der Mutter teuren Lippen,
Göttlich-unverändert-süßen,
Tönt das grausenvolle Wort:
Sohn, o Sohn! welch Übereilen!
Deiner Mutter Leichnam dorten,
Neben ihm das freche Haupt
Der Verbrecherin, des Opfers
Waltender Gerechtigkeit!
Mich nun hast du ihrem Körper
Eingeimpft auf ewige Tage:
Weisen Wollens, wilden Handelns
Werd ich unter Göttern sein;
Ja, des Himmelsknaben Bildnis
Webt so schön vor Stirn und Auge —
Senkt sichs in das Herz herunter,
Regt es tolle Wutbegier.

Immer wird es wiederkehren,
Immer steigen, immer sinken,
Sich verdüstern, sich verklären,
So hat Brahma dies gewollt.
Er gebot ja buntem Fittich,
Klarem Antlitz, schlanken Gliedern
Göttlich-einzigem Erscheinen
Mich zu prüfen, zu verführen;
Denn von oben kommt Verführung,
Wenns den Göttern so beliebt.
Und so soll ich, die Brahmane,
Mit dem Haupt im Himmel weilend,
Fühlen, Paria, dieser Erde
Niederziehende Gewalt.

Sohn, ich sende dich dem Vater!
Tröste! — Nicht ein traurig Büßen,
Stumpfes Harren, stolz Verdienen
Halt euch* in der Wildnis fest;
Wandert aus durch alle Welten,
Wandelt hin durch alle Zeiten
Und verkündet auch Geringstem:
Daß ihn Brahma droben hört!

Ihm ist keiner der Geringste —
Wer sich mit gelähmten Gliedern,
Sich mit wild zerstörtem Geiste,
Düster, ohne Hilf und Rettung,
Sei er Brahma, sei er Paria,
Mit dem Blick nach oben kehrt,
Wirds empfinden, wirds erfahren:
Dort erglühen tausend Augen,
Ruhend lauschen tausend Ohren,
Denen nichts verborgen bleibt.

Heb ich mich zu seinem Throne,
Schaut er mich, die Grausenhafte,
Die er gräßlich umgeschaffen,
Muß er ewig mich bejammern,

Euch zugute komme das.
Und ich werd ihn freundlich mahnen,
Und ich werd ihm wütend sagen,
Wie es mir der Sinn gebietet,
Wie es mir im Busen schwellet.
Was ich denke, was ich fühle —
Ein Geheimnis bleibe das.

DANK DES PARIA

Großer Brahma! nun erkenn ich,
Daß du Schöpfer bist der Welten!
Dich als meinen Herrscher nenn ich,
Denn du lässest alle gelten.

Und verschließest auch dem Letzten
Keines von den tausend Ohren;
Uns, die tief Herabgesetzten,
Alle hast du neu geboren.

Wendet euch zu dieser Frauen,*
Die der Schmerz zur Göttin wandelt!
Nun beharr ich, anzuschauen
Den, der einzig wirkt und handelt.

Paria: an outcast from Indian society. *Brahma, Brahmen*: Brahma is the supreme god of Indian religion, worshipped by Brahmins (here called 'Brahmen', but usually called 'Brahmanen' today). *Bajadere* = 'courtesan'; the sense is 'even prostitutes have a goddess'. *hohler Wirbel*: this is genitive plural. *In die Flammen*: according to former custom, Indian wives were burned alive on their husbands' funeral pyres. *Nicht ein traurig Büßen. . . halt euch*: the sense is 'let no sad atoning keep you a prisoner in the wilderness'. *zu dieser Frauen*: 'Frauen' is singular here.

Written 1821–3. Goethe recalled that he had had the theme in mind for forty years, and indeed he first read the tale on which it is based in 1783. The change that had taken place in him is typified by the fact that, whereas in 'Grenzen der Menschheit' he had regarded it as impossible for mortals to reach both heaven and earth at the same time, he now writes of one who achieves just this, and who thereby becomes a kind of saviour for the pariahs. The story has indeed some parallels with the Christian idea of salvation: the woman who is at first so pure that she has 'magical' control of the elements redeems the pariah by taking his defiled nature upon herself, or rather by having it accidentally thrust upon her. This legend is well suited

to Goethe's conviction that all that is outcast by men is acceptable to men and gods ('du lässest alle gelten'), and one guesses that he does not intend only social distinctions. Although the moral is close to his idea of the synthesis of opposites, however (see p. 49 above), it is not precisely that, for the resurrected woman, half goddess, half pariah, is a grotesque combination rather than a perfect fusion. She knows purity but continues to know carnal desires (one may bear in mind Goethe's veneration of Iphigenie at the time he was writing the *Römische Elegien*) and while she affirms that Brahma is sensitive and merciful to all, she also declares that she will denounce him to his face for the treatment he has given her. The polarity seems to extend into her vision of Brahma, it is not a seamless incarnation.

The verse moves in a rapid patter to an almost unbroken rhythm, the first and the last sections being distinguished from the rest by rhyme. The general effect is of an almost childlike chanting, and this impression is reinforced by the frequent omission of the definite article ('Füge Haupt dem Rumpfe wieder') and by the artless, 'native'-sounding language of the two men ('Was geschehen? Was verschuldet?'; 'Deine Gattin magst du töten | Aber meine Mutter nicht!'). This may be a deliberate device, 'placing' the slightly crude theology of the poem.

The legend appeals, like 'Der Gott und die Bajadere', in that it makes a plea for the outcast, and yet is not wholly satisfying since it carries the dichotomy into the heavenly realm without resolving it—and even in a way concealing it: 'Was ich denke, was ich fühle — | Ein Geheimnis bleibe das.'

The same story was used by Thomas Mann in *Die vertauschten Köpfe*.

LOVE-POEMS OF
HIS OLD AGE

LOVE-POEMS OF HIS OLD AGE

Goethe felt his life to be perennially renewed; it was a series of rebirths which went on into old age. One of the most exhilarating of these was that which began in the summer of 1814, when, nearing 65, he not only began the collection of poems now known as the *West-östlicher Divan*, but very soon fell in love with the young Marianne Jung, shortly before her marriage to his friend the Geheimrat von Willemer. In the following months Goethe lived again the kind of delight that had inspired him when he wrote 'Mailied' more than forty years before, although the ironical detachment he had known even then was still present and sometimes more acutely felt. Nine years later, now aged 74, Goethe fell in love even more irrevocably, and this time desperately, with the extraordinarily beautiful Ulrike von Levetzow, then aged seventeen. The 'Marienbader Elegie', forming the central part of what he later called the *Trilogie der Leidenschaft*, records his sense of tragic loss when he was obliged to leave Ulrike for ever.

To be in love was for Goethe never only to be in love with one woman; there was always the sense that each lover was the embodiment at this moment of an almost divine lover, as the women loved by Wilhelm Meister were all reflections of the unattainable Natalie for whom all Wilhelm's life was an intermittent search. The cosmic overtones of this love are expressed above all in 'Wiederfinden', although they are also present in 'In tausend Formen'. The almost mystical sense that goes with this is seen in the strange, barely comprehensible but suggestive poem 'Der Bräutigam'.

The *Divan* is a work of several hundred poems, of which only a few are reprinted here. In general intention, it is, as the fuller title might suggest, a further instance of Goethe's cosmic purpose: consisting to a large extent of imitations of the medieval Persian poet Hafiz, it is a work in which Goethe adopts the guise both of a European and of an Oriental, both

of a Christian and of a Muslim (however unorthodox): it is a
straddling of the globe, a deliberate adaptation to foreign ways
such as few European writers before Goethe had ever made
(Montesquieu's *Lettres Persanes* and Beckford's *Vathek* come
to mind). There is a certain sense in which Goethe not merely
sees his lovers as reflections of the divine but sees himself
too in the role of an earth-embracing deity: 'Allah braucht
nicht mehr zu schaffen, Wir erschaffen seine Welt.' The am-
bitions of his youth, in so far as Faust expressed them in the
line 'Bin ich ein Gott?', receive a strange fulfilment.

<p align="center">✶ ✶ ✶</p>

SELIGE SEHNSUCHT

Sagt es niemand, nur den Weisen,
Weil die Menge gleich verhöhnet:
Das Lebendge will ich preisen,
Das nach Flammentod sich sehnet.

In der Liebesnächte Kühlung,
Die dich zeugte, wo du zeugtest,
Überfällt dich fremde Fühlung,
Wenn die stille Kerze leuchtet.

Nicht mehr bleibest du umfangen
In der Finsternis Beschattung,
Und dich reißet neu Verlangen
Auf zu höherer Begattung.

Keine Ferne macht dich schwierig,
Kommst geflogen und gebannt,*
Und zuletzt, des Lichts begierig,
Bist du, Schmetterling,* verbrannt.

Und solang du das nicht hast,
Dieses: Stirb und werde!
Bist du nur ein trüber Gast
Auf der dunklen Erde.

gebannt: 'enthralled'. *Schmetterling*: the butterfly is an ancient symbol of the soul.

Written 31 July 1814, and included in the *Divan*. The theme of 'Flammen-tod' recurs in 'Der Gott und die Bajadere' (p. 136 above). In the present poem the poet lies awake, having just begotten a child in the same way that his father begot him ('die dich zeugte'—one must not be pedantic about the grammatical structure here). Seeing the candle-flame still alight, his thoughts turn from his satiety, and the dissatisfaction, perhaps, at this repetitive procreation, towards a higher, mystical union still conceived in a sexual sense ('höhere Begattung'). He sees himself as a butterfly or moth, fatally attracted to the candle-flame as the source of Light. But, he adds, until you have yielded to this (divine?) attraction as a lover yields, the earth will remain a place of darkness.

The rippling, almost tripping metre is characteristic of much of the *Divan*. The carefree rhyme in verse 2 is also typical of Goethe's ease of manner at this time. It is as though Goethe wanted to write of a love comparable to that in the *Song of Solomon* (which has also been interpreted mystically, and indeed mystics often do use sexual metaphors), but to do so in a strangely lighthearted seriousness. Feminine rhymes, rapidly recurring, speed on the pace (note how the masculine rhyme in verse 4, the last verse in the original version, brings the movement to a momentary close, and how the last verse of all, added later, also includes a masculine rhyme, but reintroduces movement with its final feminine one.)

'Stirb und werde!': these famous words obviously have something to do with rebirth, but 'werde!' has overtones unreproducible in English. Not just 'become something else' is meant, but also something like 'grow with the universe', 'die to selfhood and be caught up in the Spirit that moves in all events, and so rejoice in them'. The rippling movement itself can convey some of this sense.

In tausend Formen magst du dich verstecken,
Doch, Allerliebste, gleich erkenn ich dich;
Du magst mit Zauberschleiern dich bedecken,
Allgegenwärtge, gleich erkenn ich dich.

An der Zypresse reinstem, jungem Streben,
Allschöngewachsne, gleich erkenn ich dich;
In des Kanales reinem Wellenleben,
Allschmeichelhafte, wohl erkenn ich dich.

Wenn steigend sich der Wasserstrahl entfaltet,
Allspielende, wie froh erkenn ich dich;

Wenn Wolke sich gestaltend umgestaltet,*
Allmannigfaltge, dort erkenn ich dich.

An des geblümten Schleiers Wiesenteppich,
Allbuntbesternte, schön erkenn ich dich;
Und greift umher ein tausendarmger Eppich,*
O Allumklammernde, da kenn ich dich.

Wenn am Gebirg der Morgen sich entzündet,
Gleich, Allerheiternde, begrüß ich dich;
Dann über mir der Himmel rein sich ründet,
Allherzerweiternde, dann atm ich dich.

Was ich mit außerm Sinn, mit innerm kenne,
Du Allbelehrende, kenn ich durch dich;
Und wenn ich Allahs Namenhundert nenne,
Mit jedem klingt ein Name nach für dich.

gestaltend umgestaltet: the sense is that clouds are constantly taking on shapes which
just as constantly change, just as the divinity in the world does. *Eppich*: 'ivy' (more
usually 'Efeu').

Written probably between March and May 1815. From the *Divan*. Marianne
von Willemer is meant, but as with the girl in 'Mailied', or Lili Schönemann,
of whom Goethe said that where she was, Nature was, much more is im-
plied. The apotheosis suggested in the last line is no formal compliment.
 The repetitive form suggests perhaps very distantly the Persian poetic
form known as the 'ghasel'; the repetition here, however, far from lending
formality, makes the poem passionate. Goethe's serene delight was never
more whole-heartedly evident.

AN SULEIKA*

Dir mit Wohlgeruch zu kosen,
Deine Freuden zu erhöhn,
Knospend müssen tausend Rosen
Erst in Gluten untergehn.

Um ein Fläschchen zu besitzen,
Das den Ruch* auf ewig hält,

Schlank wie deine Fingerspitzen,
Da bedarf es einer Welt;

Einer Welt von Lebenstrieben,
Die, in ihrer Fülle Drang,
Ahndeten schon Bulbuls* Lieben,
Seelerregenden Gesang.

Sollte jene Qual uns quälen,
Da sie unsre Lust vermehrt?
Hat nicht Myriaden Seelen
Timurs* Herrschaft aufgezehrt?

Suleika is the Persian name by which Goethe addresses Marianne von Willemer.
Ruch: 'Geruch' (scent). Goethe uses poetic licence in omitting the prefix 'Ge-'.
Bulbul: the Persian name for the nightingale. *Timur*: Tamburlaine.

Written 27 May 1815. The poem appears in the *Divan* next to 'Der Winter
und Timur' (p. 144 above), to which it is a pendant, for the ferocity of
Tamburlaine is brought in parallel with the indifference of lovers to the
torments of rosebuds, burned in order to provide the scent which heightens
their delight in one another. The excessive scruple about the roses is not a
whim: it is rather a means, not wholly successful, of suggesting an identity
between the extremes of hatred (in Tamburlaine) and of love, a paradox
akin to those in many of Goethe's poems (see p. 49 above). With recent
German history in mind, one hardly knows how seriously to take the
parallel drawn in the last verse, which seems detestable.

An vollen Büschelzweigen,
Geliebte, sieh nur hin!
Laß dir die Früchte zeigen,
Umschalet* stachlig grün.

Sie hängen längst geballet,*
Still, unbekannt mit sich;
Ein Ast, der schaukelnd wallet,
Wiegt sie geduldiglich.

Doch immer reift von innen
Und schwillt der braune Kern,

Er möchte Luft gewinnen
Und säh die Sonne gern.

Die Schale platzt, und nieder
Macht er sich freudig los;
So fallen meine Lieder
Gehäuft in deinen Schoß.

Umschalet: 'husked round'. *längst geballet*: 'already rounded for some time'.

Written at Heidelberg (by a chestnut tree on the Schloßterrasse) on 24 September 1814, for Marianne, and included in the *Divan*. For evocative sounds, as in line 4, and rhythms, as in line 8, this is one of Goethe's most marvellous lyrics, a 'Dinggedicht', as Rilke might have called it a century later. The last two lines are not merely a formal rounding off, although clearly Goethe was much concerned with making the chestnuts live through sounds—he never calls them by their name. The brown kernels are at the same time metaphors for Goethe's poems, and only this reference really brings home the still mysterious significance of 'unbekannt mit sich' and the mood of plenitude and abundance.

ZWIESPALT

Wenn links an Baches Rand
Cupido flötet,
Im Felde rechter Hand
Mavors* drommetet,*
Da wird dorthin das Ohr
Lieblich gezogen,
Doch um des Liedes Flor*
Durch Lärm betrogen.
Nun flötets immer voll
Im Kriegesthunder,*
Ich werde rasend, toll —
Ist das ein Wunder?
Fort wächst der Flötenton,
Schall der Posaunen,
Ich irre, rase schon —
Ist das zu staunen?

Mavors is another name for Mars. *drommetet*: 'trumpets'. *des Liedes Flor*: 'the climax of the song' ('Flor' = bloom, prime, heyday). *Kriegesthunder*: 'thunder of war'.

Written 27 July 1814. The first four lines most singular in sound. 'Krieges-thunder' means 'Kriegesdonner', i.e. the second half of the word is really English. (Cp. 'bewhelmen', also in the *Divan*, though not a German word, for 'overwhelm'—a further instance of the carefree use of language already mentioned (p. 157 above. See also p. xxviii).)

VOLLMONDNACHT

Herrin, sag, was heißt das Flüstern?
Was bewegt dir leis die Lippen?
Lispelst immer vor dich hin,
Lieblicher als Weines Nippen!
Denkst du, deinen Mundgeschwistern*
Noch ein Pärchen herzuziehn?
'Ich will küssen! Küssen! sagt ich.'

Schau! Im zweifelhaften Dunkel
Glühen blühend alle Zweige,
Nieder spielet Stern auf Stern;
Und smaragden durchs Gesträuche
Tausendfältiger Karfunkel:
Doch dein Geist ist allem fern.
'Ich will küssen! Küssen! sagt ich.'

Dein Geliebter, fern, erprobet*
Gleicherweis im Sauersüßen,
Fühlt ein unglückselges Glück.
Euch im Vollmond zu begrüßen,
Habt ihr heilig angelobet;
Dieses ist der Augenblick.
'Ich will küssen! Küssen! sag ich.'

Mundgeschwistern: i.e. 'lips'. *erprobet* is a past participle: the lover is 'thoroughly tried and tested'.

Written 24 October 1815. From the *Divan*. A slave-girl speaks; her mistress answers in the refrain. Again, the sensation of kissing comes through the pure sound, while the dark colours of verse 2 glow like an enamelled Persian miniature. When the slave-girl speaks of her mistress's

lover being 'erprobet gleich im Sauersüßen' she means that he too is accustomed to this sour yet sweet delight of kissing in imagination only. ('Sour' is certainly the only meaning possible, but should not be taken too literally—the alliteration may have been the chief attraction of the word.)

WIEDERFINDEN

Ist es möglich! Stern der Sterne,
Drück ich wieder dich ans Herz!
Ach, was ist die Nacht der Ferne
Für ein Abgrund, für ein Schmerz!
Ja, du bist es, meiner Freuden
Süßer, lieber Widerpart;*
Eingedenk vergangner Leiden,
Schaudr ich vor der Gegenwart.

Als die Welt im tiefsten Grunde
Lag an Gottes ewger Brust,
Ordnet' er die erste Stunde
Mit erhabner Schöpfungslust,
Und er sprach das Wort: Es werde!*
Da erklang ein schmerzlich Ach!
Als das All mit Machtgebärde
In die Wirklichkeiten* brach.

Auf tat sich das Licht: so trennte
Scheu sich Finsternis von ihm,
Und sogleich die Elemente*
Scheidend auseinanderfliehn.
Rasch, in wilden, wüsten Träumen
Jedes nach der Weite rang,
Starr, in ungemeßnen Räumen,
Ohne Sehnsucht, ohne Klang.

Stumm war alles, still und öde,
Einsam Gott zum erstenmal!
Da erschuf er Morgenröte,*
Die erbarmte sich der Qual;

Sie entwickelte dem Trüben
Ein erklingend Farbenspiel,
Und nun konnte wieder lieben,
Was erst auseinanderfiel.

Und mit eiligem Bestreben
Sucht sich, was sich angehört;
Und zu ungemeßnem Leben
Ist Gefühl und Blick gekehrt.
Seis Ergreifen, sei es Raffen,
Wenn es nur sich faßt und hält!
Allah braucht nicht mehr zu schaffen,
Wir erschaffen seine Welt.

So, mit morgenroten Flügeln,
Riß es mich an deinen Mund,
Und die Nacht mit tausend Siegeln
Kräftigt sternenhell den Bund.
Beide sind wir auf der Erde
Musterhaft in Freud und Qual,
Und ein zweites Wort: Es werde!*
Trennt uns nicht zum zweitenmal.

Widerpart: the word means 'opponent' as well as 'complement'—perhaps Goethe
intends, paradoxically, to suggest something of both senses. *Es werde!*: 'Let there
be...'. *In die Wirklichkeiten*: the 'All' is thought of as a compact mass, which splits
up into countless fragments and thereby becomes a collection of realities, whereas
before it was absolute, not real. *Elemente*: the four elements of the ancients are
meant—earth, air, fire and water. *Morgenröte*: see commentary below.

Written 24 September 1814. From the *Divan*. The passionate beginning
shows how in Goethe's love for Marianne there was the thought that he was
finding in her the woman he had always loved. As he says in the last verse,
he first flew to her on the wings of Dawn (in his youth), now he comes
to her again in old age (die Nacht). He had been absent not from her,
but from Love—this was the 'Nacht der Ferne', rather than distance from
her, whom he had scarcely met. And remembering what suffering love
has caused him before, he knows that it will bring not only joys but also
'Leiden', at the thought of which he shudders.

This may help to explain the sudden transition in verse 2 to the creation
of the universe. Just as the created things, emanating from the All (or
rather breaking in fragments from it, as lines 15–16 say), were separate from

God from the moment that he spoke the Fiat ('Es werde!'), so Goethe was separated from his Beloved. As the creation returns to God through love, so Goethe's return to the Beloved in the person and form of Marianne renders the two lovers, as it were, divine.

The mode of this coming together is less clear. It is achieved by God alone, since he creates 'Morgenröte' (the name used by the mystic Jacob Boehme, and because of him by the German Romantics, for the 'Bride of God', and sometimes, though not by Goethe, for Christ), and in some way she makes love possible once more. The reference to a 'Farbenspiel' (the rainbow?) may have to do with Goethe's symbolical 'Theory of Colours', but has not yielded good sense to the commentators.

Further difficulty is caused by verse 5, where it seems that by love Goethe is content to mean any form of clasping or grabbing. (Cp. the Roman Elegy on p. 129 above.) The thought evoked by this, of countless savage as well as tender embraces, seems partly ironical, as though the world were being urged to accept any kind of love-making, without too much fuss. Perhaps some such paradox as that in *An Suleika* and *Der Winter und Timur* is intended. The compactness of the poem leaves much to the reader's inventiveness.

TRILOGIE DER LEIDENSCHAFT

AN WERTHER

Noch einmal wagst du, vielbeweinter Schatten,
Hervor dich an das Tageslicht,
Begegnest mir auf neu beblümten Matten,*
Und meinen Anblick scheust du nicht.
Es ist, als ob du lebtest in der Frühe,
Wo uns der Tau auf Einem Feld* erquickt,
Und nach des Tages unwillkommner Mühe
Der Scheidesonne letzter Strahl entzückt;
Zum Bleiben ich, zum Scheiden* du erkoren,
Gingst du voran — und hast nicht viel verloren.

Des Menschen Leben scheint ein herrlich Los:
Der Tag wie lieblich, so die Nacht wie groß!
Und wir, gepflanzt in Paradieses Wonne,
Genießen kaum der hocherlauchten Sonne,

Da kämpft sogleich verworrene Bestrebung
Bald mit uns selbst und bald mit der Umgebung;
Keins wird vom andern wünschenswert ergänzt,
Von außen düstert's, wenn es innen glänzt,
Ein glänzend Äußres deckt mein trüber Blick,
Da steht es nah — und man verkennt das Glück.

Nun glauben wir's zu kennen! Mit Gewalt
Ergreift uns Liebreiz weiblicher Gestalt:
Der Jüngling, froh wie in der Kindheit Flor,
Im Frühling tritt als Frühling selbst hervor,
Entzückt, erstaunt, wer dies ihm angetan?
Er schaut umher, die Welt gehört ihm an.

Ins Weite zieht ihn unbefangne Hast,
Nichts engt ihn ein, nicht Mauer, nicht Palast;
Wie Vögelschar an Wäldergipfeln streift,
So schwebt auch er, der um die Liebste schweift,
Er sucht vom Äther,* den er gern verläßt,
Den treuen Blick, und dieser hält ihn fest.

Doch erst zu früh und dann zu spät gewarnt,
Fühlt er den Flug gehemmt, fühlt sich umgarnt,
Das Wiedersehn ist froh, das Scheiden schwer,
Das Wieder-Wiedersehn beglückt noch mehr,
Und Jahre sind im Augenblick ersetzt;
Doch tückisch harrt das Lebewohl zuletzt.

Du lächelst, Freund, gefühlvoll, wie sich ziemt:
Ein gräßlich Scheiden machte dich berühmt;
Wir feierten dein kläglich Mißgeschick,
Du ließest uns zu Wohl und Weh zurück;
Dann zog uns wieder ungewisse Bahn
Der Leidenschaften labyrinthisch an;
Und wir, verschlungen wiederholter Not,
Dem Scheiden endlich* — Scheiden ist der Tod!
Wie klingt es rührend, wenn der Dichter singt,
Den Tod zu meiden, den das Scheiden bringt!

Verstrickt in solche Qualen, halbverschuldet,
Geb' ihm ein Gott zu sagen, was er duldet.

Matten: 'meadows' (usually called 'Wiesen'). *auf Einem Feld*: the capital 'E' implies emphasis. *zum Scheiden*: this refers to Werther's suicide. *Äther*...: this difficult passage may mean that the lover is like a bird darting about the tree-tops, glad of the support provided by the air or ether, yet seeking independence from it in his soaring, just as the man needs the woman and is sustained by her but also wants freedom. *Dem Scheiden endlich*: understand '*destined* to part'.

ELEGIE

Und wenn der Mensch in seiner Qual verstummt,
Gab mir ein Gott zu sagen, was ich leide.

Was soll ich nun vom Wiedersehen hoffen,
Von dieses Tages noch geschloßner Blüte?
Das Paradies, die Hölle steht dir offen;
Wie wankelsinnig regt sich's im Gemüte! —
Kein Zweifeln mehr! Sie tritt ans Himmelstor,
Zu ihren Armen hebt sie dich empor.

So warst du denn im Paradies empfangen,
Als wärst du wert des ewig schönen Lebens;
Dir blieb kein Wunsch, kein Hoffen, kein Verlangen,
Hier war das Ziel des innigsten Bestrebens,
Und in dem Anschaun dieses einzig Schönen
Versiegte gleich der Quell sehnsüchtiger Tränen.

Wie regte nicht der Tag die raschen Flügel,
Schien die Minuten vor sich her zu treiben!
Der Abendkuß, ein treu verbindlich Siegel:
So wird es auch der nächsten Sonne bleiben.
Die Stunden glichen sich in zartem Wandern
Wie Schwestern zwar, doch keine ganz den andern.

Der Kuß, der letzte, grausam süß, zerschneidend
Ein herrliches Geflecht verschlungner Minnen.*
Nun eilt, nun stockt der Fuß, die Schwelle meidend,
Als trieb' ein Cherub* flammend ihn von hinnen;

Das Auge starrt auf düstrem Pfad verdrossen,
Es blickt zurück, die Pforte steht verschlossen.

Und nun verschlossen in sich selbst, als hätte
Dies Herz sich nie geöffnet, selige Stunden
Mit jedem Stern des Himmels um die Wette
An ihrer Seite leuchtend nicht empfunden;
Und Mißmut, Reue, Vorwurf, Sorgenschwere
Belasten's nun in schwüler Atmosphäre.

Ist denn die Welt nicht übrig? Felsenwände,
Sind sie nicht mehr gekrönt von heiligen Schatten?
Die Ernte, reift sie nicht? Ein grün Gelände,
Zieht sich's nicht hin am Fluß durch Busch und Matten?
Und wölbt sich nicht das überweltlich Große,
Gestaltenreiche, bald Gestaltenlose?

Wie leicht und zierlich, klar und zart gewoben
Schwebt, seraphgleich, aus ernster Wolken Chor,
Als glich' es ihr, am blauen Äther droben,
Ein schlank Gebild aus lichtem Duft empor!
So sahst du sie in frohem Tanze walten,
Die lieblichste der lieblichsten Gestalten.

Doch nur Momente darfst dich unterwinden,
Ein Luftgebild statt ihrer festzuhalten;
Ins Herz zurück! dort wirst du's besser finden,
Dort regt sie sich in wechselnden Gestalten;
Zu Vielen bildet Eine sich hinüber,
So tausendfach* und immer, immer lieber.

Wie zum Empfang sie an den Pforten weilte
Und mich von dannauf stufenweis beglückte;
Selbst nach dem letzten Kuß mich noch ereilte,
Den letztesten mir auf die Lippen drückte:
So klar beweglich bleibt das Bild der Lieben,
Mit Flammenschrift ins treue Herz geschrieben.

Ins Herz, das fest, wie zinnenhohe Mauer,
Sich ihr bewahrt und sie in sich bewahret,
Für sie sich freut an seiner eignen Dauer,
Nur weiß von sich, wenn sie sich offenbaret,
Sich freier fühlt in so geliebten Schranken
Und nur noch schlägt, für alles ihr zu danken.

War Fähigkeit zu lieben, war Bedürfen
Von Gegenliebe weggelöscht, verschwunden,
Ist Hoffnungslust zu freudigen Entwürfen,
Entschlüssen, rascher Tat sogleich gefunden!
Wenn Liebe je den Liebenden begeistet,*
Ward es an mir aufs lieblichste geleistet;

Und zwar durch sie! — Wie lag ein innres Bangen
Auf Geist und Körper, unwillkommner Schwere:
Von Schauerbildern rings der Blick umfangen
Im wüsten Raum beklommner Herzensleere;
Nun dämmert Hoffnung von bekannter Schwelle,*
Sie selbst erscheint in milder Sonnenhelle.

Dem Frieden Gottes, welcher euch hienieden
Mehr als Vernunft beseliget — wir lesen's* —,
Vergleich' ich wohl der Liebe heitern Frieden
In Gegenwart des allgeliebten Wesens;
Da ruht das Herz, und nichts vermag zu stören
Den tiefsten Sinn, den Sinn: ihr zu gehören.

In unsers Busens Reine wogt ein Streben,
Sich einem Höhern, Reinern, Unbekannten
Aus Dankbarkeit freiwillig hinzugeben,
Enträtselnd sich den ewig Ungenannten;
Wir heißen's: fromm sein! — Solcher seligen Höhe
Fühl' ich mich teilhaft, wenn ich vor ihr stehe.

Vor ihrem Blick, wie vor der Sonne Walten,
Vor ihrem Atem, wie vor Frühlingslüften,
Zerschmilzt, so* längst sich eisig starr gehalten,
Der Selbstsinn tief in winterlichen Grüften;

Kein Eigennutz, kein Eigenwille dauert,
Vor ihrem Kommen sind sie weggeschauert.

Es ist, als wenn sie sagte: 'Stund' um Stunde
Wird uns das Leben freundlich dargeboten.
Das Gestrige ließ uns geringe Kunde,
Das Morgende, zu wissen ist's verboten;
Und wenn ich je mich vor dem Abend scheute,
Die Sonne sank und sah noch, was mich freute.

Drum tu wie ich und schaue, froh-verständig,
Dem Augenblick ins Auge! Kein Verschieben!
Begegn' ihm schnell, wohlwollend wie lebendig,
Im Handeln sei's, zur Freude sei's dem Lieben;
Nur wo du bist, sei alles, immer kindlich,
So bist du alles, bist unüberwindlich.'

Du hast gut reden, dacht' ich: zum Geleite
Gab dir ein Gott die Gunst des Augenblickes,
Und jeder fühlt an deiner holden Seite
Sich augenblicks den Günstling des Geschickes;
Mich schreckt der Wink, von dir mich zu entfernen—
Was hilft es mir, so hohe Weisheit lernen!

Nun bin ich fern! Der jetzigen Minute,
Was ziemt denn der? Ich wüßt' es nicht zu sagen;
Sie bietet mir zum Schönen manches Gute,
Das lastet nur, ich muß mich ihm entschlagen;
Mich treibt umher ein unbezwinglich Sehnen,
Da bleibt kein Rat als grenzenlose Tränen.

So quellt denn fort! und fließet unaufhaltsam;
Doch nie geläng's, die innre Glut zu dämpfen!
Schon rast's und reißt in meiner Brust gewaltsam,
Wo Tod und Leben grausend sich bekämpfen.
Wohl Kräuter gäb's, des Körpers Qual zu stillen;
Allein dem Geist fehlt's am Entschluß und Willen,

Fehlt's am Begriff: wie sollt' er sie vermissen?
Er wiederholt ihr Bild zu tausendmalen.

Das zaudert bald, bald wird es weggerissen,
Undeutlich jetzt und jetzt im reinsten Strahlen;
Wie könnte dies geringstem Troste frommen,
Die Ebb' und Flut, das Gehen wie das Kommen?

Verlaßt mich hier, getreue Weggenossen!
Laßt mich allein am Fels, in Moor und Moos;
Nur immer zu! euch ist die Welt erschlossen,
Die Erde weit, der Himmel hehr und groß;
Betrachtet, forscht, die Einzelheiten sammelt,
Naturgeheimnis werde nachgestammelt.

Mir ist das All, ich bin mir selbst verloren,
Der ich noch erst den Göttern Liebling war;
Sie prüften mich, verliehen mir Pandoren, *
So reich an Gütern, reicher an Gefahr;
Sie drängten mich zum gabeseligen Munde,
Sie trennen mich, und richten mich zu Grunde.

Minnen: 'Minne' in medieval German meant 'love'; the word was reintroduced
about 1770 by the poets of the 'Göttinger Hain' but has fallen out of use again.
ein Cherub: cp. Gen. iii. 24. *tausendfach*: cp. 'In tausend Formen', p. 157 above.
begeistet: not, apparently, 'begeistert', 'fills with enthusiasm', but a special word,
meaning perhaps 'makes into Spirit'. *Schwelle*: the threshold of the East, where
the sun rises, is meant. *wir lesen's*: cp. Phil. iv. 7. *so* is a relative pronoun, meaning
'der'. *Pandora*, the first woman on earth according to Greek mythology, was
endowed by the gods with every gift, but presented her husband with a box
which, when opened, released all manner of evils.

AUSSÖHNUNG

Die Leidenschaft bringt Leiden! — Wer beschwichtigt,
Beklommnes Herz, dich, das zu viel verloren?
Wo sind die Stunden, überschnell verflüchtigt?
Vergebens war das Schönste dir erkoren!
Trüb' ist der Geist, verworren das Beginnen;
Die hehre Welt, wie schwindet sie den Sinnen!

Da schwebt hervor Musik mit Engelsschwingen,
Verflicht zu Millionen Tön' um Töne,

Des Menschen Wesen durch und durch zu dringen,
Zu überfüllen ihn mit ew'ger Schöne:
Das Auge netzt sich, fühlt im höhern Sehnen
Den Götter-Wert der Töne wie der Tränen.

Und so das Herz erleichtert merkt behende,
Daß es noch lebt und schlägt und möchte schlagen,
Zum reinsten Dank der überreichen Spende
Sich selbst erwidernd willig darzutragen.
Da fühlte sich — o daß es ewig bliebe! —
Das Doppel-Glück der Töne wie der Liebe.

TRILOGIE DER LEIDENSCHAFT. The three poems were actually written in
the reverse order to that in which they are arranged, the first in March 1824,
the second in September 1823, the third in August 1823. The 'Aussöhnung'
or resolution is thus poetical rather than biographical, although the connection
between the poems makes them a unity. Goethe's account, recorded by
Eckermann under 1 December 1831, is slightly inaccurate in respect of the
order of composition.

An Werther. Although this poem is often highly esteemed, it perhaps
betrays a temporary inability in Goethe to face the past, which in any case he
as a rule preferred to forget, in order to face the present and future more
boldly. The gesture towards form may be significant here: the way in
which the first verse tends towards the *ottava rima*, whereas later verses are
merely rhymed couplets in groups of different lengths. The contrast
between this and the form of the much greater 'Elegie' which follows
suggests a certain negligence.

There is negligence in the thought, too. The poem is a confrontation with
the spirit of Werther, the hero of Goethe's youthful novel, for a jubilee
edition of which he had been asked to write an introduction. It is thus a
confrontation with suicide, as Goethe recognizes with some irony when he
addresses the younger man as 'vielbeweint' (the reference is to the highly
sentimental reception which the novel received). This detachment quickly
gives way, however, to an oppressive melancholy which sees only dis-
illusionment in all experience. Some of the sadness here is self-indulgently
pessimistic, as when Goethe affirms that inward happiness is always accom-
panied by outward disasters, while the sequence of thought in verse 5
sounds disjointed. One has the impression here of a man so downcast
at the thought of Werther's suicide that he can pay full attention neither to
form nor to content.

In the last verse, however, the tone changes—Werther seems almost to
be mocked with the word 'gefühlvoll', which hits off the very quality that

171

drove him to take his own life, until the almost absurd bathos of 'kläglich Mißgeschick' introduces a doubt whether Goethe has any firm purpose at all. (A 'lamentable misfortune' is an odd misnomer for Werther's death.) The thought proceeds to no particular end, but rather moves into an abrupt, half self-pitying, half angry complaint that the poet is still alive enough to suffer. (The last line of all is a reminiscence of that spoken by Tasso in Goethe's play of that name, and quoted—with 'was' instead of 'wie'—at the head of 'Elegie'.) Goethe gives us a confused view of the various emotions stirred in him by Werther, not a clear-eyed movement towards understanding them or mastering them, such as is found, *mutatis mutandis*, in the 'Dejection' and 'Immortality' odes of Coleridge and Wordsworth.

Elegie. Goethe treasured this poem (often called 'Marienbader Elegie') more than any other of his old age. Written in the coach leaving Marienbad, where he had fallen in love with Ulrike vom Levetzow, it is in places the most moving and human of them all. It is important to know that in the MS the first verse was written on a separate page with a line underneath, indicating that it is a complete thought in itself rather than one which leads on to the rest. (Goethe is saying that 'she'—the beloved who appears, now as Helen does to Faust, now as Natalie does to Wilhelm Meister—will receive him in heaven despite his present loss.)

In the following verses Goethe reviews his condition, weaving together his memories of the real Ulrike and all that she meant to him beyond herself, but much more delicately and clearly than in 'Wiederfinden'. He has been driven from Paradise like a second Adam; he tries to console himself with earthly beauty and memories of Ulrike (a similar image to that of the cloud in verse 7 is used for Helen in *Faust*, Act IV); he attempts to recall the wise joy of 'In tausend Formen', and to see again in Ulrike the 'Morgenröte' of the poem 'Wiederfinden'; he tells himself that love is like the peace of God, and allows Ulrike to remind him of his own philosophy of the intense experience of the moment in joy or sorrow, and of his confidence in the eternal goodness of God (the sun, he says, 'sah noch, was mich freute'—that is, even when the sun had set for him, Goethe, it was still glorying in all the sights that had at one time or another rejoiced him. The thought that the sun can never see shadows always had great symbolical weight for Goethe). But all this wisdom is worthless to him in his present state; nothing can replace the living presence of the Beloved herself. The thought of taking some opiate occurs, but is dismissed, and Goethe ends with two verses (also separated off in the MS by a line, like the first verse) in which he tells his companions (either in his spiritual quest or in the coach at the time of writing) to go on without him. The gods have granted him knowledge of Pandora, the Eve of Greek mythology who brought men not only delight but great misery, and he is left now irrevocably in the wilderness. None of Goethe's poems has so unrelievedly tragic a sense as this.

Aussöhnung. Written originally for the Polish pianist Marie Szymanowska,

this now rounds off the Trilogy as a 'reconciliation', being linked to the 'Elegie' by its verse-form. Despite the quickening movement of the last verse, however, it is difficult to see more than a vague idea of music as 'uplifting' (rather as poetry is said to be in 'Zueignung', p. 67 above), and the echoing of the second verse in the last line of the third verse seems formal rather than meaningful.

DER BRÄUTIGAM*

Um Mitternacht, ich schlief, im Busen wachte*
Das liebevolle Herz, als wär es Tag;
Der Tag erschien, mir war, als ob es nachte —
Was ist es mir, so viel er bringen mag?

Sie fehlte ja!* mein emsig Tun und Streben
Für sie allein ertrug ichs durch die Glut
Der heißen Stunde; welch erquicktes Leben
Am kühlen Abend! lohnend war's und gut.

Die Sonne sank, und Hand in Hand verpflichtet
Begrüßten wir den letzten Segensblick,
Und Auge sprach, ins Auge klar gerichtet:
Von Osten, hoffe nur, sie kommt zurück.

Um Mitternacht, der Sterne Glanz geleitet
Im holden Traum zur Schwelle,* wo sie ruht.
O sei auch mir dort auszuruhn bereitet!
Wie es auch sei, das Leben, es ist gut.

Der Bräutigam: there may be mystical overtones here (Christ as the Bridegroom?). *ich schlief, im Busen wachte...*: cp. the Song of Solomon, v. 2 ('Ich schlafe aber mein Herz wacht'). *Sie fehlte ja!*: 'she would be absent' (even though it were day). *Schwelle*: cp. the use of this word in verse 12 of 'Elegie' (p. 168 above) and footnote on p. 170.

Written not earlier than 1826, but perhaps later, since there may be a reference in verse 3 to Charlotte von Stein, who died in January 1827, and to whom Goethe usually referred in his diaries by the astrological symbol for the Sun.

A mysterious poem, which may yield meaning along some such lines as these. The poem is about the whole of Goethe's life, in which he has always been aware of a flame of (divine?) love, so luminous as to render

ordinary light trivial. For the sake of this love he has borne with life, and the evening of his days has been refreshed by it. Moreover, there have been lovers in his life who represented this higher love to him; they may have vanished like the sun, but one may be confident that like the sun love will return. Meanwhile, the poet hopes that at death he may join the loving Sun at the threshold where dawn rises; yet with all that, life is good.

This does not explain all the poem, especially not the title, for if Christ is meant to be thought of here, the speaker can be no mortal man. Perhaps, however, Goethe allows some diffuseness of meaning here.

The movement of the verse is alive with a variety of moods, from the passionate sweep-through of verse 2 to the resonant gratitude of 'lohnend' at the end of that verse and the confident assertion of the final line.

POETRY OF
WISDOM

POETRY OF WISDOM

'The wisdom of a human being resides as much in silence as in speech,' writes T. S. Eliot in his essay 'Goethe as the Sage' (in *On Poetry and Poets*), and nobody need expect wisdom to be reducible to an aphorism or so, or expect it to be any the wiser for being set out at length. Goethe's wisdom is partly sheer mystery, like the strange landscape of 'Wo hast du das genommen', partly a matter of paradox and ambiguity, like all wisdom since the oracle of Delphi, and just as open to objection and criticism. The bald statement of contradictories as though both were equally true can be irritating, yet most prophets and philosophers have been driven into making such an utterance, or have done so unconsciously. We probably do best to remain dissatisfied with such paradoxes, and to be reconciled to them, if at all, only in the awareness that the best poetry does sometimes point towards something rather like them, as does *The Phoenix and Turtle* of Shakespeare. 'Thoughts that do lie too deep for tears' can never be directly expressed, and perhaps the paradox is at best a distortion of the inexpressible.

* * *

'Wo hast du das genommen?
Wie konnt es zu dir kommen?
Wie aus dem Lebensplunder
Erwarbst du diesen Zunder,
Der Funken letzte Gluten
Von frischem zu ermuten?'

Euch mög es nicht bedünkeln,
Es sei gemeines Fünkeln;
Auf ungemeßner Ferne,
Im Ozean der Sterne,
Mich hatt ich nicht verloren,
Ich war wie neugeboren.

Von weißer Schafe Wogen
Die Hügel überzogen,
Umsorgt von ernsten Hirten,
Die gern und schmal* bewirten,
So ruhig-liebe Leute,
Daß jeder mich erfreute.

In schauerlichen Nächten,
Bedrohet von Gefechten;
Das Stöhnen der Kamele
Durchdrang das Ohr, die Seele,
Und derer, die sie führen,
Einbildung und Stolzieren.

Und immer ging es weiter,
Und immer ward es breiter,
Und unser ganzes Ziehen,
Es schien ein ewig Fliehen,
Blau, hinter Wüst und Heere,
Der Streif erlogner Meere.

schmal: 'frugally' (usual sense: 'narrowly').

Written before 30 May 1815, and included in the *Divan*, this is to be understood as a reply to those who ask whence the poet derives so much inspiration in his old age. He answers that although in his spirit he was like a man adrift in an ocean of stars (one thinks of Faust's venture across trackless oceans in quest of the 'Mothers', in Act I of Part II), he had not lost possession of himself, and thus was as though reborn into the strange, celestial, yet Oriental, landscape which he now describes. The mysterious spreading horde of the last verse is perhaps our clue to the state of mind in which Goethe's aged creativity arose.

UM MITTERNACHT

Um Mitternacht ging ich, nicht eben gerne,
Klein, kleiner Knabe, jenen Kirchhof hin
Zu Vaters Haus, des Pfarrers; Stern am Sterne,
Sie leuchteten doch alle gar zu schön;
 Um Mitternacht.

Wenn ich dann ferner in des Lebens Weite
Zur Liebsten mußte, mußte, weil sie zog,
Gestirn und Nordschein* über mir im Streite,
Ich gehend, kommend Seligkeiten sog;
 Um Mitternacht.

Bis dann zuletzt des vollen Mondes Helle
So klar und deutlich mir ins Finstere drang,
Auch der Gedanke willig, sinnig, schnelle
Sich ums Vergangne wie ums Künftige schlang;
 Um Mitternacht.

Nordschein: the 'aurora borealis'.

Written 13 February 1818, in what Goethe later called 'ein wunder-
samer Zustand bei hehrem Mondenschein', this bears the marks of spon-
taneous composition, being quite ungrammatical, though none the less
comprehensible for that. The little boy of verse 1 may seem not to be
meant for Goethe, in that his father is a parson, but the words 'Vaters Haus'
perhaps have Biblical overtones, and Goethe may mean he was going 'to
his Father's house'. The chief unity consists in the increase in the intensity
of the light from verse to verse, the moon itself appearing as it were in
diapason. (Cp. 'Dem aufgehenden Vollmonde', p. 193 below.) The sensation
of past and present being fused in one, which accompanies this enlighten-
ment, is described by Goethe in *Dichtung und Wahrheit*, book 14—'eine
Anschauung,' he says, 'die etwas Gespenstermäßiges in die Gegenwart
brachte'. The refrain has a mysterious ambiguity. (See the longer account
in my *Introduction to German Poetry*, p. xvii.)

URWORTE. ORPHISCH

ΔAIMωN, *Dämon*

Wie an dem Tag, der dich der Welt verliehen,
Die Sonne stand* zum Gruße der Planeten,
Bist alsobald und fort und fort gediehen
Nach dem Gesetz, wonach du angetreten.
So mußt du sein, dir kannst du nicht entfliehen,
So sagten schon Sibyllen, so Propheten;
Und keine Zeit und keine Macht zerstückelt
Geprägte Form, die lebend sich entwickelt.

ΤΥΧΗ, *Das Zufällige*

Die strenge Grenze doch umgeht gefällig
Ein Wandelndes, das mit und um uns wandelt;
Nicht einsam bleibst du, bildest dich gesellig,
Und handelst wohl so, wie ein andrer handelt:
Im Leben ist's bald hin-, bald widerfällig,
Es ist ein Tand und wird so durchgetandelt.
Schon hat sich still der Jahre Kreis geründet,
Die Lampe harrt der Flamme, die entzündet.

ΕΡΩΣ, *Liebe*

Die bleibt nicht aus! — Er stürzt vom Himmel nieder,
Wohin er sich aus alter Öde schwang,
Er schwebt heran auf luftigem Gefieder
Um Stirn und Brust den Frühlingstag entlang,
Scheint jetzt zu fliehn, vom Fliehen kehrt er wieder:
Da wird ein Wohl im Weh, so süß und bang.
Gar manches Herz verschwebt im Allgemeinen,
Doch widmet sich das edelste dem Einen.

ΑΝΑΓΚΗ, *Nötigung*

Da ist's denn wieder, wie die Sterne wollten:
Bedingung und Gesetz; und aller Wille
Ist nur ein Wollen, weil wir eben sollten,*
Und vor dem Willen schweigt die Willkür stille;
Das Liebste* wird vom Herzen weggescholten,
Dem harten Muß bequemt sich Will' und Grille.
So sind wir scheinfrei denn, nach manchen Jahren
Nur enger dran, als wir am Anfang waren.

ΕΛΠΙΣ, *Hoffnung*

Doch solcher Grenze, solcher eh'rnen Mauer
Höchst widerwärt'ge Pforte wird entriegelt,
Sie stehe nur mit alter Felsendauer!
Ein Wesen regt sich leicht und ungezügelt:

Aus Wolkendecke, Nebel, Regenschauer
Erhebt sie uns, mit ihr, durch sie beflügelt,
Ihr kennt sie wohl, sie schwärmt durch alle Zonen —
Ein Flügelschlag — und hinter uns Äonen!

Die Sonne stand: according to astrologers, a man's life is destined by the relationship
of the sun to the planets at his birth. Goethe did not believe in astrology, but some-
times toyed half-seriously with it. *weil wir eben sollten*: although we think we have
free will, we are obliged to will what we ought and are thus *not* free. *Das Liebste*:
devoted to one lover, we may find ourselves obliged to drive away another.

Written 7–8 October 1817; Goethe later published a commentary. The title
refers to the primal concepts of the Orphic religion (of which the centre was
Orpheus), but there is a typically Goethean sense in the sequence whereby
the restrictive Daimon (the unchangeable element in human nature, the
old Adam, as Goethe explained) is followed by the liberating Chance,
just as expansion follows contraction in the heart (cp. 'Im Atemholen...',
p. 188 below). The concept of polarity (p. 49 above) operates here. In
the Eros of the third verse there is, Goethe says, a momentary fusion of the
preceding two, ending, however, in restriction once again, which does not
end till the new liberation of Hope in verse 5. A kind of alternating pulse
runs through the whole.

The *ottave rime* are used here with greater significance than in 'Zueig-
nung' (p. 67 above), the couplets rounding off the thought in each verse.
One notices also how informal the language now is: 'Die bleibt nicht aus!';
'Da ist's denn wieder'; 'enger dran', etc. There is an easy nonchalance now,
and a confidential way of addressing the reader that contrasts well with the
earlier poem.

DAUER IM WECHSEL

Hielte diesen frühen Segen,
Ach, nur Eine Stunde fest!*
Aber vollen Blütenregen
Schüttelt schon der laue West.
Soll ich mich des Grünen freuen,
Dem ich Schatten erst verdankt?
Bald wird Sturm auch das zerstreuen,
Wenn es falb im Herbst geschwankt.

Willst du nach den Früchten greifen,
Eilig nimm dein Teil davon!

Diese fangen an zu reifen,
Und die andern keimen schon;
Gleich mit jedem Regengusse
Ändert sich dein holdes Tal,
Ach, und in demselben Flusse
Schwimmst du nicht zum zweitenmal.

Du nun selbst! Was felsenfeste
Sich vor dir hervorgetan,
Mauern siehst du, siehst Paläste
Stets mit andern Augen an.
Weggeschwunden ist die Lippe,
Die im Kusse sonst genas,
Jener Fuß, der an der Klippe
Sich mit Gemsenfreche* maß.

Jene Hand, die gern und milde
Sich bewegte, wohlzutun,
Das gegliederte Gebilde,
Alles ist ein andres nun.
Und was sich an jener Stelle
Nun mit deinem Namen nennt,*
Kam herbei wie eine Welle,
Und so eilts zum Element.

Laß den Anfang mit dem Ende
Sich in Eins zusammenziehn!
Schneller als die Gegenstände
Selber dich vorüberfliehn!
Danke, daß die Gunst der Musen
Unvergängliches verheißt,
Den Gehalt in deinem Busen
Und die Form in deinem Geist.

Hielte...fest: i.e. 'if only this wealth of blossoms might remain one single hour'.
Gemsenfreche: 'the temerity of a chamois'. *Und was sich...nennt*: i.e. 'the physical
body which is still called by your name has no more permanence than a wave'.

Written 1801-3. The rhythm catches the reader up into a kaleidoscopic
image of transience, in which nothing retains its present form for more than

an instant, and even the river, which retains the same general appearance, is constantly being replaced by new waters. Since even we ourselves change as the river does, there seems to be no escape from an ultimate identity with all things in which individuality perishes (cp. the end of *Faust II*, Act III). The last verse, however, proposes a remedy: these rapid changes may either be seen as a circle rotating round the still centre of one's self, so that beginning and end are indistinguishable, or (Goethe may have meant) they may contract into a single point—in each case the rapid sweep may be viewed from a secure recess of indestructible selfhood—there is 'permanence in change', as the title has it.

The connection of these thoughts with the last four lines is hard to see; the 'Gehalt' would seem to be equivalent to the circling phenomena of life, while the 'Form' must presumably correspond to the centre of selfhood, but it does not become clear how these two provide something imperishable, in contrast with the earlier verses. It is perhaps significant in this connection that the rhythm and rhyme-scheme continue to race on at the end as though no whole solution, reflected in sound as well as sense, had been found.

EPIRRHEMA

Müsset im Naturbetrachten
Immer eins wie alles achten:
Nichts ist drinnen, nichts ist draußen;
Denn was innen, das ist außen.
So ergreifet ohne Säumnis
Heilig öffentlich Geheimnis.

———

Freuet euch des wahren Scheins,
Euch des ernsten Spieles:
Kein Lebendiges ist ein Eins,
Immer ist's ein Vieles.

Written 1819. The title is the name given to a part of the chorus in Greek drama: its significance here is not clear. The poem is illuminated by Goethe's remark that to speak of an optical 'illusion' is blasphemy—things look as they are meant to look. Also present is Goethe's conception of the paradoxical fusion of opposites, extending here to the pattering, almost chatting presentation of quite serious thoughts—an 'ernstes Spiel', in fact.

EINS UND ALLES

Im Grenzenlosen sich zu finden,
Wird gern der Einzelne verschwinden,
Da löst sich aller Überdruß;
Statt heißem Wünschen, wildem Wollen,
Statt läst'gem Fordern, strengem Sollen
Sich aufzugeben ist Genuß.

Weltseele, komm, uns zu durchdringen!
Dann mit dem Weltgeist selbst zu ringen,
Wird unsrer Kräfte Hochberuf.
Teilnehmend führen gute Geister,
Gelinde leitend, höchste Meister,
Zu dem, der alles schafft und schuf.

Und umzuschaffen das Geschaffne,
Damit sich's nicht zum Starren waffne,
Wirkt ewiges, lebendiges Tun.
Und was nicht war, nun will es werden
Zu reinen Sonnen, farbigen Erden;
In keinem Falle darf es ruhn.

Es soll sich regen, schaffend handeln,
Erst sich gestalten, dann verwandeln;
Nur scheinbar steht's Momente still.
Das Ewige regt sich fort in allen:
Denn alles muß in Nichts zerfallen,
Wenn es im Sein beharren will.

VERMÄCHTNIS

Kein Wesen kann zu nichts zerfallen!
Das Ew'ge regt sich fort in allen,
An Sein erhalte dich beglückt!
Das Sein ist ewig: denn Gesetze
Bewahren die lebend'gen Schätze,
Aus welchen sich das All geschmückt.

Das Wahre war schon längst gefunden,
Hat edle Geisterschaft verbunden;
Das alte Wahre, faß es an!
Verdank es, Erdensohn, dem Weisen,*
Der ihr,* die Sonne zu umkreisen,
Und dem Geschwister* wies die Bahn.

Sofort nun wende dich nach innen:
Das Zentrum findest du da drinnen,
Woran kein Edler zweifeln mag.
Wirst keine Regel da vermissen:
Denn das selbständige Gewissen
Ist Sonne deinem Sittentag.

Den Sinnen hast du dann zu trauen,
Kein Falsches lassen sie dich schauen,
Wenn dein Verstand dich wach erhält.
Mit frischem Blick bemerke freudig
Und wandle, sicher wie geschmeidig,
Durch Auen reichbegabter Welt.

Genieße mäßig Füll' und Segen;
Vernunft sei überall zugegen,
Wo Leben sich des Lebens freut.
Dann ist Vergangenheit beständig,
Das Künftige voraus lebendig,
Der Augenblick ist Ewigkeit.

Und war es endlich dir gelungen,
Und bist du vom Gefühl durchdrungen:
Was fruchtbar ist, allein ist wahr —
Du prüfst das allgemeine Walten,
Es wird nach seiner Weise schalten,
Geselle dich zur kleinsten Schar.

Und wie von alters her, im stillen,
Ein Liebewerk nach eignem Willen

Der Philosoph, der Dichter schuf,
So wirst du schönste Gunst erzielen:
Denn edlen Seelen vorzufühlen*
Ist wünschenswertester Beruf.

dem Weisen: Copernicus (1473–1543), who taught that the planets move round the sun, not round the earth, as was then believed. *ihr* refers to 'Erde' in the word 'Erdensohn' in the preceding line; the usage is strained. *dem Geschwister*: the moon or the moon and the planets. *vorzufühlen*: the sense may be that to write down such thoughts as noble souls of later generations will come to feel as true is a most desirable occupation.

The first of these two poems was written in October 1821, the second—to correct a false impression the first had caused—in February 1829.

The poems present complementary, sometimes deliberately contradictory, but ultimately identical views. Whereas 'Eins und Alles' asserts the need to give up the 'being' one has, in order to be penetrated with the 'World-Soul', 'Vermächtnis' replies that no one can give up 'Being', since that is precisely what the World-Soul is. The paradox can thus be sorted out, and yet should not become too plain, for there is a sense in which the two kinds of 'Sein' coalesce.

The later verses of 'Vermächtnis' are hard to follow. The link between the image of earth and moon circling the sun, and the conscience as a sun to the will and desires, is clear; it is less clear why, in verse 4, the senses are said to be now thoroughly trustworthy, or why in later verses the knowledge of the requirements of conscience leads to such happiness. (Cp. the lines in *Faust* 'Der gute Mensch in seinem dunklen Drange | Ist sich des rechten Weges wohl bewußt', which similarly imply that to know the requirements of conscience is enough—the matter of fulfilling the requirements is not mentioned.) Later verses seem to be rather the formulae of Goethe's experience than communications of his insights, verse 6 being particularly abrupt in its transitions. By contrast with, say, 'Um Mitternacht', one feels the drag of words here.

ALLERDINGS

DEM PHYSIKER

'*Ins Innre der Natur*' —
O du Philister! —
'*Dringt kein erschaffner Geist.*'
Mich und Geschwister

186

Mögt ihr an solches Wort
Nur nicht erinnern!
Wir denken: Ort für Ort
Sind wir im Innern.
'*Glückselig, wem sie nur*
Die äußre Schale weist!'
Das hör ich sechzig Jahre wiederholen,
Ich fluche drauf, aber verstohlen;
Sage mir tausend tausendmale:
Alles gibt sie reichlich und gern;
Natur hat weder Kern
Noch Schale,
Alles ist sie mit einemmale.
Dich prüfe du nur allermeist,
Ob du Kern oder Schale seist.

Written *c.* 1819. The words in inverted commas are from the early eighteenth-century Swiss poet Haller. The point of the whole is close to that of *Epirrhema*: we can be 'outside' ourselves, observing our behaviour, and yet know that we are still somehow inside ourselves too.

SPRÜCHE

Wär' nicht das Auge sonnenhaft,
Die Sonne könnt' es nie erblicken;
Läg' nicht in uns des Gottes eigne Kraft,
Wie könnt' uns göttliches entzücken?

* * *

Was wär ein Gott, der nur von außen stieße,
Im Kreis das All am Finger laufen ließe!
Ihm ziemt's, die Welt im Innern zu bewegen,
Natur in Sich, Sich in Natur zu hegen,
So daß, was in Ihm lebt und webt und ist,
Nie Seine Kraft, nie Seinen Geist vermißt.

* * *

Willst du ins Unendliche schreiten,
Geh nur im Endlichen nach allen Seiten.

* * *

Was der Mensch als Gott verehrt,
Ist sein eigenstes Innere herausgekehrt.

*　　*　　*

Im Atemholen sind zweierlei Gnaden:
Die Luft einziehen, sich ihrer entladen;
Jenes bedrängt, dieses erfrischt;
So wunderbar ist das Leben gemischt.
Du danke Gott, wenn er dich preßt,
Und dank ihm, wenn er dich wieder entläßt.

*　　*　　*

Wie einer ist, so ist sein Gott;
Darum ward Gott so oft zu Spott.

*　　*　　*

All unser redlichstes Bemühn
Glückt nur im unbewußten Momente.
Wie möchte denn die Rose blühn,
Wenn sie der Sonne Herrlichkeit erkennte!

*　　*　　*

Wenn im Unendlichen dasselbe
Sich wiederholend ewig fließt,
Das tausendfältige Gewölbe
Sich kräftig ineinander schließt,
Strömt Lebenslust aus allen Dingen,
Dem kleinsten wie dem größten Stern,
Und alles Drängen, alles Ringen
Ist ewige Ruh in Gott dem Herrn.

*　　*　　*

Erkenne dich! — Was soll das heißen?
Es heißt: Sei nur! und sei auch nicht!
Es ist eben ein Spruch der lieben Weisen,
Der sich in der Kürze widerspricht.

There are several hundred 'Sprüche' among the works of Goethe's old
age. Most of them were written between 1810 and 1820. Those reproduced
here are concerned with Goethe's neo-Platonist belief in the mutual inter-
penetration of God and man and in the identity of opposites.

POEMS OF HIS
OLD AGE

Dämmrung senkte sich von oben,
Schon ist alle Nähe fern;
Doch zuerst emporgehoben
Holden Lichts der Abendstern!
Alles schwankt ins Ungewisse,
Nebel schleichen in die Höh';
Schwarzvertiefte Finsternisse
Widerspiegelnd ruht der See.

Nun im östlichen Bereiche
Ahn ich Mondenglanz und -Glut,
Schlanker Weiden Haargezweige
Scherzen auf der nächsten Flut.
Durch bewegter Schatten Spiele
Zittert Lunas Zauberschein,
Und durchs Auge schleicht die Kühle
Sänftigend ins Herz hinein.

The supreme work among fourteen short poems in the *Chinesisch-Deutsche Jahres- und Tageszeiten*, all written in 1827, and forming one more of Goethe's attempts at intuitive knowledge of foreign cultures (cp. his imitations of Roman, Greek and Persian forms). The complex meaning of the images, all conveying serenity at the thought of oncoming darkness, is reflected in the setting by Othmar Schoeck.

Weiß wie Lilien, reine Kerzen,
Sternen gleich, bescheidner Beugung,
Leuchtet aus dem Mittelherzen
Rot gesäumt, die Glut der Neigung.

So frühzeitige Narzissen
Blühen reihenweis im Garten.
Mögen wohl die guten wissen,
Wen sie so spaliert* erwarten.

spaliert: 'drawn up in a line' (not 'on a trellis', as is sometimes meant).

Another of the *Chinesisch-Deutsch* poems, less Chinese in feeling but vivid in its picture, the compact 'Glut der Neigung' playing on both the colour of the heart and the sexual attractiveness of the flower; the second verse tame by comparison, with its little joke. 'Bescheidner Beugung' means 'of modest (humble) curvature', but sounds more beautiful than that rendering.

FRÜHLING ÜBERS JAHR*

Das Beet, schon lockert
Sich's in die Höh',
Da wanken Glöckchen
So weiß wie Schnee;
Safran entfaltet
Gewalt'ge Glut,
Smaragden keimt es
Und keimt wie Blut.
Primeln stolzieren
So naseweis,
Schalkhafte Veilchen,
Versteckt mit Fleiß;
Was auch noch alles
Da regt und webt,
Genug, der Frühling,
Er wirkt und lebt.

Doch was im Garten
Am reichsten blüht,
Das ist des Liebchens
Lieblich Gemüt.
Da glühen Blicke
Mir immerfort,
Erregend Liedchen,
Erheiternd Wort;
Ein immer offen,
Ein Blütenherz,
Im Ernste freundlich
Und rein im Scherz.

Wenn Ros' und Lilie
Der Sommer bringt,
Er doch vergebens
Mit Liebchen ringt.

Frühling übers Jahr: 'Spring all the year through'.

Written probably in March 1816. Again a vivid first verse followed by an ordinary and somewhat conventional one. Cp. 'Im Herbst 1775' (p. 33).

DEM AUFGEHENDEN VOLLMONDE

DORNBURG, 25. AUGUST 1828

Willst du mich sogleich verlassen?
Warst im Augenblick so nah!
Dich umfinstern Wolkenmassen,
Und nun bist du gar nicht da.

Doch du fühlst, wie ich betrübt bin,
Blickt dein Rand herauf als Stern!
Zeugest mir, daß ich geliebt bin,
Sei das Liebchen noch so fern.*

So hinan denn! hell und heller,
Reiner Bahn, in voller Pracht!
Schlägt mein Herz auch schmerzlich schneller,
Überselig ist die Nacht.

noch so fern: 'however far away'.

Sent to Marianne von Willemer. The moon, which had always been so meaningful for Goethe, here grows into the full symbol of his love. Cp. 'An den Mond' (p. 34), 'Um Mitternacht' (p. 178).

Hätte Gott mich anders gewollt,
So hätt er mich anders gebaut;
Da er mir aber Talent gezollt,
Hat er mir viel vertraut.

Ich brauch' es zur Rechten und Linken,
Weiß nicht, was daraus kommt;
Wenn's nicht mehr frommt,
Wird er schon winken.

The exact date of this humorous expression of gratitude and familiarity is
not known. The sense recalls the phrase 'wie wahr, wie seiend!' (p. 125).

Am Jüngsten Tag,* vor Gottes Thron
Stand endlich Held Napoleon.
Der Teufel hielt ein großes Register
Gegen denselben und seine Geschwister,
War ein wundersam verruchtes Wesen;
Satan fing an, es abzulesen.

Gott Vater, oder Gott der Sohn,
Einer von beiden sprach vom Thron,
Wenn nicht etwa gar der Heilige Geist
Das Wort genommen allermeist:

'Wiederhols nicht vor göttlichen Ohren!
Du sprichst wie die deutschen Professoren.
Wir wissen alles, mach es kurz!
Am Jüngsten Tag ists nur ein.
Getraust du dich, ihn anzugreifen,
So magst du ihn nach der Hölle schleifen.'

Am Jüngsten Tag: 'on the day of Judgment'.

A piece of vulgarity and blasphemy of a kind Goethe had always indulged
in from time to time, the so-called 'Walpurgissack' often being the recipient.
The missing word is 'Furz'. The last two lines are oddly inconclusive.

Im ernsten Beinhaus war's, wo ich beschaute,
Wie Schädel Schädeln angeordnet paßten;
Die alte Zeit gedacht ich, die ergraute.

Sie stehn in Reih' geklemmt, die sonst sich haßten,
Und derbe Knochen, die sich tödlich schlugen,
Sie liegen kreuzweis, zahm allhier zu rasten.
Entrenkte Schulterblätter! was sie trugen,
Fragt niemand mehr, und zierlich-tät'ge Glieder,
Die Hand, der Fuß, zerstreut aus Lebensfugen.
Ihr Müden also lagt vergebens nieder,
Nicht Ruh' im Grabe ließ man euch, vertrieben
Seid ihr herauf zum lichten Tage wieder,
Und niemand kann die dürre Schale lieben,
Welch herrlich edlen Kern sie auch bewahrte.
Doch mir Adepten war die Schrift geschrieben,
Die heil'gen Sinn nicht jedem offenbarte,
Als ich inmitten solcher starren Menge
Unschätzbar herrlich ein Gebild gewahrte,
Daß in des Raumes Moderkält* und Enge
Ich frei und wärmefühlend mich erquickte,
Als ob ein Lebensquell dem Tod entspränge.
Wie mich geheimnisvoll die Form entzückte!
Die gottgedachte Spur, die sich erhalten!
Ein Blick, der mich an jenes Meer* entrückte,
Das flutend strömt gesteigerte Gestalten.
Geheim Gefäß! Orakelsprüche spendend,
Wie bin ich wert, dich in der Hand zu halten?
Dich höchsten Schatz aus Moder fromm entwendend
Und in die freie Luft, zu freiem Sinnen,
Zum Sonnenlicht andächtig hin mich wendend.
Was kann der Mensch im Leben mehr gewinnen,
Als daß sich Gott-Natur ihm offenbare?
Wie sie das Feste läßt zu Geist verrinnen,
Wie sie das Geisterzeugte fest bewahre.

Moderkält(-e): 'mouldering cold'. *jenes Meer*: perhaps the Aegean, the 'gesteigerte Gestalten' being the figures of ancient Greeks.

Written September 1829. Goethe gave the poem no title, but it has been known both as 'Schillers Reliquien' and 'Bei Betrachtung von Schillers Schädel', and these titles certainly reflect his intention, for all that Schiller

is not mentioned by name. Unlike Hamlet with the skull of Yorick, Goethe does not see in the bones a *memento mori*, and scarcely recalls the man to whom they belonged. The stately form of the *terza rima*, Dante's measure in the Divine Comedy, is deliberately chosen, for the occasion is one that austerely enhances Goethe's delight in living. One perhaps needs to recall the enthusiasm for anatomy which Goethe had had since he was a young man, and his early belief in physiognomy, to appreciate how the fine shape of a skull could give him such excitement. More than this, however, it is an object-lesson in the paradoxes he was always proclaiming in his old age. The spirit, he implies in the final lines, has been rarefied from the flesh that once imprisoned it, and yet the very fineness of the spirit has left its trace in the mortal remains: the skull is so striking because the man himself was. This is the very expression of 'Gott-Natur'—not of Nature alone nor of God alone, but of that which is both at once. It is the visible evidence that death serves life.

INDEX OF
TITLES AND BEGINNINGS OF POEMS

Alternative titles are given in square brackets

Adler und Taube	page 50
All unser redlichstes Bemühn	188
Allerdings	186
Alles geben die Götter	115
Am Jüngsten Tag, vor Gottes Thron	194
An Belinden	12
An den Geist des Johannes Secundus	20
An den Mond	34
An die Türen will ich schleichen	117
An Schwager Kronos	52
An Suleika	158
An vollen Büschelzweigen	159
An Werther	164
Anmutig Tal! du immergrüner Hain!	59
Auf Christianen R.	10
[*Auf dem See*]	32
Auf Kieseln im Bache, da lieg' ich	7
Aus dem Tagebuch der Reise in die Schweiz	32
Aussöhnung	170
Balde seh ich Rickchen wieder	9
Bedecke deinen Himmel, Zeus	45
Bedenk, o Kind!	78
[*Bei Betrachtung von Schillers Schädel*]	194
Beispiel	80
Chinesisch-Deutsche Jahres- und Tageszeiten	191–2
[*Christel*]	11
Cophtisches Lied	130
Cupido, loser, eigensinniger Knabe!	130
Da hatt ich einen Kerl zu Gast	77
Dämmrung senkte sich von oben	191
Das Beet, schon lockert sich's	192
Das Göttliche	93

Das Veilchen	page 101
Das Wasser rauscht', das Wasser schwoll	105
Dauer im Wechsel	181
Dem aufgehenden Vollmonde	193
Dem Geier gleich	55
Dem Schnee, dem Regen, dem Wind entgegen	19
Der Bräutigam	173
Der du von dem Himmel bist	115
Der Fischer	105
Der Gott und die Bajadere	136
Der König in Thule	102
Der Morgen kam; es scheuchten seine Tritte	67
Der untreue Knabe	108
Der Winter und Timur	144
Der Zauberlehrling	140
Des Menschen Seele gleicht dem Wasser	87
Die Leidenschaft bringt Leiden!	170
Die Nebel zerreißen	38
[*Diner zu Koblenz*]	78
Dir mit Wohlgeruch zu kosen	158
Edel sei der Mensch	93
Ein Adlersjüngling hob die Flügel	50
Ein anderes (Cophtisches Lied)	131
[*Ein gleiches (Wanderers Nachtlied)*)]	37
Ein Veilchen auf der Wiese stand	101
Eins und Alles	184
Elegie	166
Epirrhema	183
Erkenne dich! — Was soll das heißen?	188
Erlkönig	106
Erschaffen und Beleben	80
Erwache, Friederike	7
Es schlug mein Herz, geschwind zu Pferde!	5
Es war ein Buhle frech genung	108
Es war ein König in Thule	102
Fetter grüne, du Laub	33
Freudvoll und leidvoll	114
Frühling übers Jahr	192
Füllest wieder Busch und Tal	34
Ganymed	48
Geh! gehorche meinen Winken	131

Genialisch Treiben	page 81
Gesang der Geister über den Wassern	87
Glückliche Fahrt	38
Grenzen der Menschheit	91
Gretchen am Spinnrad	103
Groß ist die Diana der Epheser	143
Großer Brahma, Herr der Mächte!	146
Gut, brav, mein Herr!	54
Gute Nacht an Annetten, da sie heuratete	75
Hab oft einen dummen düstern Sinn	10
Hans Adam war ein Erdenkloß	80
Harfenspieler	116, 117
Harzreise im Winter	55
Hat der alte Hexenmeister	140
Hätte Gott mich anders gewollt	193
Heidenröslein	100
Heiß mich nicht reden, heiß mich schweigen	120
[Herbstgefühl]	33
Herbstlich leuchtet die Flamme	128
Herrin, sag, was heißt das Flüstern?	161
Herz, mein Herz, was soll das geben	12
Hielte diesen frühen Segen	181
Ich saug' an meiner Nabelschnur	32
Ich wollt, ich wär ein Fisch	25
Ilmenau	59
Im Atemholen sind zweierlei Gnaden	188
Im ernsten Beinhaus war's	194
Im Grenzenlosen sich zu finden	184
Im Herbst 1775	33
In tausend Formen magst du dich verstecken	157
'Ins Innre der Natur'	186
Ist doch keine Menagerie	14
Ist es möglich! Stern der Sterne	162
Katechisation	78
Kein Wesen kann zu nichts verfallen	184
Kenner und Künstler	54
Kennst du das Land	118
Kleine Blumen, kleine Blätter	4
Laß dich, Geliebte, nicht reun	129
Lasset Gelehrte sich zanken und streiten	130

Liebebedürfnis	page 21
Lieber, heiliger, großer Küsser	20
Liebhaber in allen Gestalten	25
Lilis Park	14
Mahadöh, der Herr der Erde	136
Mahomets-Gesang	42
[*Maifest*]	30
Mailied	30
[*Marienbader Elegie*]	166
Meeres Stille	38
Meine Göttin	89
Meine Ruh' ist hin	103
Mignon	118, 119, 120, 121
Mit einem gemalten Band	4
Müsset im Naturbetrachten	183
Nach Mittage saßen wir	76
Neue Liebe, neues Leben	12
Noch einmal wagst du, vielbeweinter Schatten	164
Nur wer die Sehnsucht kennt	119
O fände für mich	75
Paria	146
Prometheus	45
Rastlose Liebe	19
Rezensent	77
Römische Elegien	128, 129
Saget, Steine, mir an	128
Sagt es niemand, nur den Weisen	156
Sah ein Knab ein Röslein stehn	100
[*Schillers Reliquien*]	194
Seht den Felsenquell	42
Selige Sehnsucht	156
So laßt mich scheinen, bis ich werde	121
So umgab sie nun der Winter	144
So wälz ich ohne Unterlaß	81
Sprüche	187
Spude dich, Kronos!	52
Stirbt der Fuchs, so gilt der Balg	76

Tiefe Stille herrscht im Wasser *page* 38
Trilogie der Leidenschaft 164
Trocknet nicht 34

Über allen Gipfeln 37
Um Mitternacht 178
Um Mitternacht ging ich 178
Um Mitternacht, ich schlief 173
Unbeständigkeit 7
Urworte. Orphisch 179

Vermächtnis 184
Vollmondnacht 161
Vom Berge 13
Vom Vater hab ich die Statur 82
Von wem ich's habe, das sag' ich euch nicht 110
Vor Gericht 110

Wandrers Nachtlied (Der du von dem Himmel bist) 115
Wandrers Nachtlied (Über allen Gipfeln) 37
Wär' nicht das Auge sonnenhaft 187
Warum gabst du uns die tiefen Blicke 22
Warum ziehst du mich unwiderstehlich 12
Was der Mensch als Gott verehrt 188
Was soll ich nun vom Wiedersehen hoffen 166
Was wär ein Gott, der nur von außen stieße 187
[*Wechsel*] 7
Weiß wie Lilien, reine Kerzen 191
Welch ein lustiges Spiel! 82
Welcher Unsterblichen 89
Wenn der uralte, heilige Vater 91
Wenn ich, liebe Lili, dich nicht liebte 13
Wenn ich mal ungeduldig werde 80
Wenn im Unendlichen dasselbe 188
Wenn links an Baches Rand 160
Wenn man zwanzig Freier zählet 75
Wer nie sein Brot mit Tränen aß 116
Wer reitet so spät 106
Wer sich der Einsamkeit ergibt 116
Wer vernimmt mich? 21
West-östlicher Divan 80, 144, 156, 157, 158, 159, 160, 161,
 162, 177
Wie an dem Tag, der dich der Welt verliehen 179
Wie einer ist, so ist sein Gott 188

Wie herrlich leuchtet *page* 30
Wie im Morgenglanze 48
Wiederfinden 162
Willkommen und Abschied 5
Willst du ins Unendliche schreiten 187
Willst du mich sogleich verlassen? 193
Wo hast du das genommen? 177
Wonne der Wehmut 34
Wunsch eines jungen Mädchens 75

Zu Ephesus ein Goldschmied saß 143
'Zu Goethes Denkmal was zahlst du jetzt?' 82
Zueignung 67
Zwiespalt 160
Zwischen Lavater und Basedow 78